Becky's new book, No Mountain Imm[ovable is an] engaging read. It takes us on a journe[y to] live a more effective life of faith in Jesus. Its central theme, that it is not so much about increasing your amount of faith, but rather activating the faith that you already have, builds with each chapter.

Becky unpacks Hebrews 11 in a digestible and engaging way. She draws deeply from a wealth of Scriptures, as well as relating her own life experiences, particularly as a missionary in Uganda and Liberia. This book is the product of a deep understanding of Scripture, but also of having lived out the principles it teaches.

I found the extensive study material at the end of each chapter especially helpful in getting the most out of this book. The study material is not simply a recap of what has just been read, but provides further and deeper insight. I would especially recommend this book for small groups to work through.

Leon Mileham
Senior Pastor, Connect Church Maidstone

More than just another book on faith, an inspirational journey, an outstanding read with excellent study guides.

Andrew H. Smith
Author and Retired Pastor

I love the fact that Becky chose to write about real life stories of common people in the Bible whom the Lord used.

She brings out these stories so well in a conversational way that helps the readers to enjoy interacting with her. For those of us who know her, it is as though she is physically sharing with us. I have enjoyed the testimonies and personal experiences because they help the readers to connect the Bible to their day-to-day life.

The discussion questions are also very helpful and get the reader to apply the message to themselves.

I pray that whoever reads this book will take the lesson seriously to help them live the life.

Thank you so much, Becky, for this gift to the body of Christ..

Peter Kasirivu
Senior Pastor, Gaba Community Church
Founder and Director, Africa Renewal Ministries

NO MOUNTAIN IMMOVABLE

HOW TO ACTIVATE YOUR FAITH

BECKY WATERMAN

NO MOUNTAIN IMMOVABLE: HOW TO ACTIVATE YOUR FAITH

Copyright © 2023 by Becky Waterman

All rights reserved. No part of this publication may be reproduced, stored in a retrieval system, or transmitted in any form or by any means, electronic, mechanical, photocopying, recording or otherwise, without the prior written consent of the publisher. Short extracts may be used for review purposes.

Unless otherwise stated, scripture quotations are taken from The Holy Bible, New International Version®, NIV®, copyright © 1973, 1979, 1984, 2011 by Biblica, Inc. Used by permission of Hodder & Stoughton Ltd. All rights reserved. 'NIV' is a registered trademark of Biblica. UK trademark number 1448790.

Scripture quotations marked NLT are taken from The Holy Bible, New Living Translation copyright © 1996, 2004, 2015 by Tyndale House Foundation. Used by permission of Tyndale House Publishers Inc., Carol Stream, Illinois 60188. All rights reserved.

Scripture quotations marked MSG are taken from The Message, copyright © 1993, 2002, 2018 by Eugene H. Peterson. Used by permission of NavPress. All rights reserved. Represented by Tyndale House Publishers.

ISBN: 9798858994848

*For every member of every small group
I've ever called home.*

ACKNOWLEDGEMENTS

No book is completed in isolation, and I am beyond thankful to those who have cheered me on throughout this process.

The concept of this book was birthed many years ago, though it looked somewhat different through its various iterations. The small chapter of Hebrews 11 caught my eye and tugged at my heart, and made me ponder what a life of faith really looks like. It began with a series of short blog posts, considering each faith-filled character in turn, and morphed into a full, three-month Bible study with a group of women, living and serving in Uganda, the country I called home at the time. I wholeheartedly thank each and every one of those wonderful women, who were willing guinea pigs for this study, and for their ongoing encouragement, out of which came the idea to produce this as a book, for others to enjoy.

There are not enough words to express my appreciation to my parents, diligent beta readers and fact checkers, and my greatest cheerleaders in every task to which I set my hand. I love you both dearly.

To Pete and Lucy, my second set of parents, your encouragement and prayers keep me going, and I am so thankful that you are a part of my life.

To Angela and Brett, Sarah and Toby, and the rest of my wonderful family. Thank you for always cheering me on.

There are too many friends to name, but you know who you are. Those who have sent messages of encouragement, who have championed my Bible teaching ministry, who have expressed their desire to get their hands on a copy of this book at last – your kind words and generosity have made this a reality. To those I have known for years, and those who have entered my days more recently, to those scattered throughout the towns and countries I have called home over the years, to those I have only had the privilege of knowing through technology; I cannot overstate the impact you have had on me. 1 Thessalonians 5:11 describes you all: *Encourage one another and build each other up, just as in fact you are doing.* Never stop.

My good friend and fellow author, Sue, you have no idea how much you inspire me to keep putting finger to keyboard to write, in one way or another. Your passion for your craft is contagious.

Thank you to those who were willing to cast an eye over this work in pre-release, to provide wonderful quotes and further encouragement to keep going. I appreciate you sparing me your very precious time.

And finally, thank you to Dave. You are the one who puts up with me at my worst and my best, and who pushes me to live up to my potential. This adventure of life has been a rollercoaster, and there's no one I'd rather ride it with.

TABLE OF CONTENTS

Acknowledgements _____ i

How to Use This Book _____ 1

Introduction: The Adventure of Faith _____ 3

Abel: The Heart of Worship _____ 17

Enoch: The Walk of Faith _____ 33

Noah: Faith in Action _____ 47

Abraham: Faith in the Unknown _____ 63

Sarah: Faith Through the Wait _____ 79

Abraham: The Testing of Faith _____ 93

Isaac: Generational Faith _____ 107

Jacob: Faith to Finish Well _____ 123

Joseph: Faith for the Future _____ 139

Moses' Parents: Faith in the Darkest Days _____ 153

Moses: The Comfort of Faith _____ 167

The Israelites: Faith in the Battle _ _ _ _ _ _ _ _ _ _ _ 183

Rahab: Saved Through Faith _ _ _ _ _ _ _ _ _ _ _ _ _ _ _ _ 199

Conclusion: Persevering in Faith _ _ _ _ _ _ _ _ _ _ _ _ 213

References _ 223

About the Author _ 225

HOW TO USE THIS BOOK

> *For the word of God is alive and active. Sharper than any double-edged sword, it penetrates even to dividing soul and spirit, joints and marrow; it judges the thoughts and attitudes of the heart.*
>
> **-Hebrews 4:12-**

The Bible is exciting. It is unlike any other book you will ever read. It is living and active, and it has the power to transform your life. It is a book you can read a hundred times, a thousand times, spotting something different within its pages each time you open the cover. When you come to the Bible expecting to hear from God, you will never be disappointed. In your reading you will uncover nuggets of wisdom, you will learn more of God's character, nature and goodness, and you will find your faith activated as you hear his voice more clearly, through his written word.

My hope, as you read this book, is that you will be inspired to dig deeper into God's word for yourself. Resources such as this can help us to grow and develop as Christians, but they are no substitute for the Bible itself.

For this reason, I have included questions for further study at the end of each chapter. They are designed to help you consider what you have read, and how it fits within Scripture at large. You can work through these questions alone, pondering and delving more deeply into how these stories relate to your life today, or you can work through them with a small group and discuss your findings together.

I have intentionally left spaces for you to scribble your thoughts within these sections. You can leave your own mark on this copy of *No Mountain Immovable;* I give you permission to scribble all over it (unless you are reading a digital copy; I accept no liability for encouraging you to draw all over your Kindle or phone! A notebook will suffice).

Thank you for joining me on this exciting adventure in the Bible. I trust this book will encourage you, and, I hope, challenge you, as you explore the living and active word of Almighty God.

INTRODUCTION
THE ADVENTURE OF FAITH

I wonder if you've ever said to yourself, 'I wish I had a little more faith.'

You wouldn't be alone. In fact, you'd be in good company. One day, Jesus was teaching his disciples the importance of forgiving a fellow believer, even if they have sinned against you seven times in one day and each time come crawling back, begging for repentance.

Clearly the disciples found this a challenge, because their response was to say to the Lord, 'Increase our faith!'[1] In other words, that's impossible! What sort of a saint would I have to be in order to be that forgiving? This is not something I can do on my own; I'm going to need a faith boost to achieve that goal.

We've all been there. I need extra faith to do this task. I need extra faith to believe for this miracle. I need extra faith to get through this terrible time in my life. Lord, increase my faith.

Faith is an interesting little word. A dictionary definition tells us it means, 'Complete trust or confidence in someone or something.' That doesn't need to be in a religious context. The example Google provided of faith being used in a sentence was, 'This restores one's faith in politicians.' I'm not sure what the 'this' was, but it must have been something incredible!

Complete, all-consuming trust and confidence in God is perhaps a good place to start when it comes to defining Christian faith, though.

All too often, we put the emphasis the other way around. Instead of thinking about who we're putting our trust and confidence in, we make it all about us and what we need to do to attain a certain level of faith. If I only prayed more, read the Bible more, gave more money, believed harder, then I could be better, more like those super-Christians who have the amazing experiences with God that I've read about. All too often, we end up disappointed and discouraged, because that's not how faith works. We're not on a sliding scale of faith, trying to attain the next rank – level five for managing to forgive that annoying person, level eight for seeing a healing miracle, level ten for a big evangelistic crusade.

It may sound controversial, but I say to you today that you don't need more faith: you need to learn to activate the faith you already have.

When the disciples asked Jesus to increase their faith, he didn't come back with a tick list of things they needed to do to reach the next faith level. He didn't even agree that they needed more faith. He said this:

> *"If you have faith as small as a mustard seed, you can say to this mulberry tree, 'Be uprooted and planted in the sea,' and it will obey you."*
>
> -Luke 17:6-

A mustard seed is one to two millimetres in diameter. It is tiny, miniscule, the smallest seed a first-century farmer in that part of the world would have known. With that level of faith, Jesus said, you can do the impossible; you can uproot a tree by speaking to it. In a similar account in the book of Matthew, Jesus explains:

> *"Truly I tell you, if you have faith as small as a mustard seed, you can say to this mountain, 'Move from here to there,' and it will move. Nothing will be impossible for you."*
>
> -Matthew 17:20-

Faith is not about anything we do; it's about knowing the person we are putting our trust and confidence in. Through him, nothing is impossible. Through him, any mountain can be moved, no matter how insurmountable or immovable it may seem.

That's easy enough to say, of course, but as you stand at the bottom of the mountain, looking up at its cloud-covered peak, it can feel utterly overwhelming. I've been there; I'm sure you have too. And I wonder, what mountains do you face even now? Sickness? Bereavement? Fear for the future? Pressure to act in a certain way? A God-given dream that seems unattainable? A series of catastrophes? Of unrelenting dark days, leaving you so overshadowed by the horror that you can't imagine a way out? Those circumstances, those mountains, certainly feel immovable as we stand at their feet.

I was eighteen years old the first time I ever flew in an aeroplane, travelling to Albania for my first experience of an overseas short-term mission trip. Even now, many years later, I can remember seeing the mighty mountain range, the

Alps, from high above through the plane's small window. I was entranced; the beauty and awe of those mountains laid out beneath me. In that instant, I was struck by how small they seemed. My elevated perspective had flattened those monstrous masses into a smooth canvas.

As we soar on wings like eagles,[2] our perspective shifts in much the same way. We continue to appreciate the scale of the mountain, I was still aware that the largest of those European peaks stretched their snow-covered tips more than 15,000 feet into the air, and yet, we see that the mountain is not everything. We recognise that our God is greater than any challenge we face; that he has the power to move even the most immovable rock.

This is why those activities – prayer, Bible study and other Christian disciplines – are so important, not because they are things we have to tick off to meet our faith-building quota for the day, but because they are activities that let us draw closer to God, to know more about him, to remind ourselves of the impossible things he is fully able to do.

That's what this book is all about.

In Hebrews 11 we are introduced to the Hall of Faith, a long list of ordinary characters who, 'by faith', did extraordinary things. I was always curious as to why God would have singled out these particular people, warts and all, to be commended as examples of what it means to live by faith. I invite you to join me in that discovery, because in each of their stories there are clues for us today in our own journeys of faith. When you start to dig into the backgrounds of these characters, how flawed and very human they tended to be, and yet how God worked incredible wonders through them, you can't help but be inspired.

> *"Without faith it is impossible to please God, because anyone who comes to him must believe that he exists and that he rewards those who earnestly seek him."*
>
> **-Hebrews 11:6-**

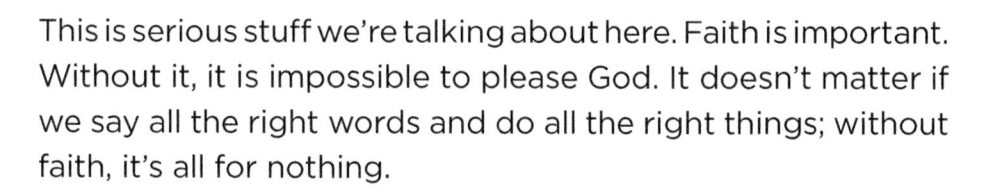

This is serious stuff we're talking about here. Faith is important. Without it, it is impossible to please God. It doesn't matter if we say all the right words and do all the right things; without faith, it's all for nothing.

I'm assuming, if you're here and reading this book, that you have some level of belief that God exists. It's a very strange phenomenon that we can believe that truth, and we can trust in an eternal life when we die, and yet struggle to believe God could meet our needs here and now. It's all too easy to doubt God's ability to help us with the little (or the large), everyday things in our lives; this mountain's a bit too big, I think, or God's surely not interested in helping me with something so small. Yet this verse tells us we can believe that he rewards those who sincerely seek him.

This adventure in faith is exciting!

However, as we've already established, we all have moments where we feel it's an area where we're lacking. Why is that?

Why is it, if there aren't levels of faith to attain, that when the disciples were desperately trying to drive out a demon and failing horrendously, Jesus told them it was because they had so little faith? Why is it that Jesus, twice, commended people for their 'great faith?' Once, when a Roman centurion pleaded for the healing of his servant, and once when a terribly ill woman reached out a shaking hand to tentatively touch the hem of Jesus' robe.

On a dark and stormy night, the twelve hand-picked disciples of Jesus were buffeted by wind and waves in their small boat. Seeing Jesus walking toward them on the water, they panic. 'It's a ghost,' they cry out in fear! And yet Peter, hearing the voice of Jesus, emboldened by him to take courage, steps onto the water and begins to walk toward his Lord. But suddenly, all he sees around him are the waves; perhaps a wave comes between him and Jesus and he loses sight of his Saviour. He starts to sink. The water flows over him, threatening to pull him under, but then there's a hand, drawing him up to safety.

> *"You of little faith," he [Jesus] said, "why did you doubt?"*
>
> **-Matthew 14:31-**

Peter, the only disciple to step out of the boat while the others remained in the place that was comfortable and (relatively) safe, the only disciple to break the laws of physics, is told he has little faith.

I don't think Peter had forgotten who Jesus was in that moment. I don't think his position on the faith ladder had dropped down a rung or two. I think in that moment, where his focus turned from his God to his circumstances, his faith didn't shrink – it vanished; it was deactivated by his doubt. In looking at the waves that threatened to drown him, and the wind that threatened to topple him, Peter had become distracted from the one thing that had the power to save him.

Does that sound familiar? You may not have a literal walking-on-water experience, but have there ever been moments where, even after taking a bold step of faith, you've suddenly found yourself questioning everything and wondering if you're in entirely the wrong place? Have financial issues, sickness or a feeling of not knowing what God is calling you to do caused you to doubt? Have you found yourself dwelling on your circumstances in your mind, rather than filling your thoughts with what God says about the situation?

Your faith may well have been deactivated in those moments.

The centurion and the sick woman Jesus commended for having great faith were entirely focussed on him. They knew who he was. They knew he had the power to heal and to save. Did they have more faith than Peter? More faith than the disciples struggling with a problematic demon (despite having dealt with similar situations in the past)? No, of course not. But their faith in that moment was active; they saw the situations, didn't deny the problems, but instead of doubting, they put their trust in the God who is bigger than the mountains that needed to be moved.

This is wonderfully encouraging. If you believe in God, you already have all the faith you need to walk boldly through any storms life throws at you. The storms will come, the moments of doubt will come, but we have a choice in how we will respond to them. We can choose to keep our minds and our hearts focussed on God. As we study the Bible's heroes of faith, we'll see what they did, and learn lessons for shoring up our own belief so we can keep our eyes firmly fixed on Jesus, even when the waves are crashing around us.

When I look back over my life, it's tempting to say that my faith has grown. At the time of writing this book, I'm a missionary serving in Liberia with Mission Aviation Fellowship. That's not always an easy life. If I had been faced with some of the experiences I've encountered in this journey when I was ten years younger, I'm not sure how well I would have coped. But when I really think about it, is it my faith which has grown? Or my knowledge of who God is, and my assurance that he will come through for me, seen with first-hand experience? Honestly, I'm not sure, but I do know that the most important thing to realise is that if faith does grow, it doesn't grow by our own efforts, but through a deep relationship with God, and through learning more of his character, and through the encouragement of the testimonies of people who have lived lives of faith and seen God move in incredible ways on their behalf.

I would love to be able to say that I never suffer from a lack of faith, that I never struggle with the situations I face, that I absolutely do count painful, testing situations as pure joy. I'm not quite there yet, and that's okay. We are all on a journey. God is the pioneer and the perfecter of our faith; we're not finished yet, but we've started. And the great news is that we can build ourselves up in the things of God every day, to minimise those moments where we find our faith lacking.

We are beyond spoilt as New Testament believers. All of the examples given to us in Hebrews 11 are found in the Old Testament, living in a time prior to Jesus coming, and sending the Holy Spirit to personally live with each believer. These people had to go on what they'd heard about God in the past, or the things they'd seen happen, or those incredibly rare occasions when God would speak directly through an angel or with his voice or through a prophet. These people did not have the same constant access to God that we have today, and yet they were commended for their incredible faith.

What's our excuse? So often we find ourselves defeated by the voices shouting at us, or by the circumstances we find ourselves in, when we literally have God within us. That's not something to be discouraged about, but it is important to ask the question: in all areas of my existence, am I really living a life of faith? If not, don't despair.

> *"Faith comes from hearing the message, and the message is heard through the word about Christ."*
>
> **-Romans 10:17-**

Diving into the word about Christ, the Bible, is a wonderful way to reactivate our faith.

Each chapter in this book comes with some questions and thoughts to help you delve deeper into what God is saying to you on this topic. I encourage you to think about them either on your own or in a group. Come with an expectation to hear God speak through his word. There's nothing that activates faith more than that.

Questions for Further Study

How would you define faith?

Read through the whole chapter of Hebrews 11.

What are your first thoughts about this chapter of the Bible?

What do the verses you have just read make you think about faith?

Is there any one verse or one character that jumped out at you? If so, why?

Does anything you have just read change your definition of what faith is?

_____
_____
_____
_____
_____

Hebrews 12:2 describes Jesus as the 'pioneer and perfecter of our faith.' What does that mean?

_____
_____
_____
_____
_____

Read Matthew 8:23-27.

Imagine yourself in the position of the disciples; they were caught in the midst of a furious storm. This wasn't a big, stable boat with a nice cabin. It would have been mostly open to the elements, with waves crashing over them, the wind blowing them off course. Water would have been flooding the bottom of the boat, and as they desperately tried to bail it out, there was Jesus, asleep.

How would you have felt if you were one of the disciples in this situation?

Why does Jesus accuse them of having 'little faith'?

What should they have seen in Jesus as he calmly slept through the storm?

How does this apply to us? Do we have 'little faith' when we get scared by the situations we face?

Think about your life. Are there any situations you are facing right now where you feel like the disciples in their boat?

How can you practically turn your gaze back onto Jesus in those situations?

Look up the following verses. For each verse, record something you can practically do to activate your faith.

Romans 10:17	
Hebrews 12:1-2	
1 Corinthians 16:13-14	
2 Corinthians 5:6-9	
Ephesians 6:16	
James 2:26	

Although the disciples were terrified, in fear of their lives, and lacking in faith at that moment, Jesus still delivered them from the storm. He didn't demand faith of a certain level in order to rescue them, he simply stepped in and did it. Even if you feel that your faith is lacking today, Jesus still promises to be with you, to help you and to guide you. Instead of worrying about how small your faith may be, focus on how great your God is, and put into place one faith-building activity this week from your list. It could be taking action and doing something God is calling you to do, getting stuck into his word, or anything else that turns your focus back to him.

ABEL

THE HEART OF WORSHIP

Welcome to the book of Genesis.

This first book of the Bible is where eight of the heroes of faith listed in Hebrews 11 find their home. It's where we encounter God's first interactions with humanity. It all starts with a man called Adam and a woman called Eve, created by God to walk with him beneath the cool trees in the Garden of Eden, to find fulfilment and pleasure, work and rest, in the company of the Almighty.

Sadly, it doesn't last long.

It's a familiar story. The serpent tempts Eve with the promise of becoming like God, knowing good and evil in all their fullness, and both she and Adam succumb. As a result, they are removed from the garden, removed from the physical presence of God, and they begin lives of toil and joy and hardship and happiness and all those things which are part of the human condition today.

In the midst of it all, Eve gives birth to her first two children: Cain and his younger brother Abel.

In all honesty, when I first started delving into this study of Hebrews 11, I questioned why Abel was included at all. Granted, chronologically he would be in first place, being one of the first four people to tread the face of the earth, but it seems as though he doesn't really do very much to be worth the great commendation of being our first example of a life lived by faith. And yet, the more I dug into this man and the little we know of his life, the more I started to realise what an exciting example he is for us today, and the more challenged I felt to consider the attitude of my own heart.

> *By faith Abel brought God a better offering than Cain did. By faith he was commended as righteous, when God spoke well of his offerings. And by faith Abel still speaks, even though he is dead.*
>
> **-Hebrews 11:4-**

In Abel's rather tragic story, he and his brother both bring an offering to God. While the Lord looks with favour on Abel's choice morsels from his flocks, the same can't be said of the fruits of the soil Cain offered. Cain grows angry at the negative reception of what he brings, and he ends up taking his brother out to the field, where he attacks and kills him. The first murder. The first death. It doesn't take long for Adam and Eve to witness the evil they were promised first hand.

Adam and Eve's children weren't quite as fortunate as their parents; they never had the joy of physically encountering God and taking a casual stroll through the garden. They never even saw the garden. Their first experience of God would have been hearing the stories their parents told them. It's only after these events occur, after Adam and Eve have another son named Seth, that we hear:

> *At that time people began to call on the name of the LORD.*
>
> **-Genesis 4:26-**

We don't know if God entered the scene here and specifically told Cain and Abel to bring an offering to him, or whether it was simply an idea they had to present a sacrifice to this awesome God their parents once knew. Either way, it seems unlikely they had much frame of reference to know what Almighty God would appreciate by way of an offering. We have no record of Adam and Eve being instructed to present anything to God, so as far as we know, this is the first time anything like this is done. Unlike the Israelites in later years who had very specific instructions regarding all they were to offer, this feels like a more impromptu decision. It was something they wanted to do, something that was a desire of their hearts, to give something back to the God who had given them life.

This is where we start to recognise why it is so crucial that Abel is included within the list, and why his example can help us to exercise our own faith muscles.

The first person commended for his faith is highlighted because he chose to bring an offering. He chose to worship God. He chose to offer something that cost him personally, in order to bring glory to the Lord.

> *And Abel also brought an offering—fat portions from some of the firstborn of his flock.*
>
> **-Genesis 4:4-**

Not only was Abel willing to give up the firstborn of his flock, but also the fat portions, the choicest bits of the meat. He wouldn't get to eat those tasty morsels himself, or trade them on for other goods. He wouldn't get to breed the firstborn of his flocks to increase their population, to increase his own wealth. Abel wasn't offering the cast-offs, the leftovers; he was giving the best of the best. His worship was a sacrifice. He was willing to surrender his very best to God, and so he was commended as righteous.

This begs the question, if Abel had such great faith for bringing his offering, why didn't Cain? He brought something too. Was God only interested in an offering of something living? That would seem to be contradicted by the fact that the books of the law specifically talk about grain offerings. The book of Leviticus even refers to a grain offering as:

> *A most holy part of the food offerings presented to the LORD.*
>
> **-Leviticus 2:10-**

That sounds like a perfectly suitable offering.

Could it be because meat was a more valuable commodity than whatever plant-based offering Cain made? Was the monetary value of Cain's offering not as high as Abel's? If that was the case then Jesus' story of a poor widow offering two tiny copper coins at the temple treasury wouldn't make much sense.

> *Calling his disciples to him, Jesus said, "Truly I tell you, this poor widow has put more into the treasury than all the others. They all gave out of their wealth; but she, out of her poverty, put in everything—all she had to live on."*
>
> **-Mark 12:43-44-**

It wouldn't have mattered how much monetary value there was associated with Cain's gift. God wouldn't have minded if Cain was simply poorer than Abel and had less to offer. We don't need to compare what we can bring to God with what other people are bringing. It doesn't matter if our tithe is less than someone else's. It doesn't matter if our singing voice isn't quite as perfect as the person standing next to us in church on a Sunday morning as we worship.

What matters is the attitude of our hearts. We see this time and again throughout the Bible.

> *"Does the LORD delight in burnt offerings and sacrifices as much as in obeying the LORD? To obey is better than sacrifice, and to heed is better than the fat of rams."*
>
> **-1 Samuel 15:22-**

> *For I desire mercy, not sacrifice, and acknowledgment of God rather than burnt offerings.*
>
> **-Hosea 6:6-**

> *You do not delight in sacrifice, or I would bring it; you do not take pleasure in burnt offerings. My sacrifice, O God, is a broken spirit; a broken and contrite heart you, God, will not despise*
>
> **-Psalm 51:16-17-**

God knows our hearts. He looked deeper than the plate of vegetables that Cain offered to him and saw the real motivation behind it. Perhaps Cain wanted nothing more than to be praised. Perhaps he was trying to compete with his brother. Perhaps he wanted to keep the best for himself and presented a plate of wilted lettuce. We don't know exactly what went on there, but we do know that God looked at the two men and deemed the offering of one acceptable, and the offering of the other unacceptable.

What a great reminder to us to check our own motivation. I wonder what spiritual offerings we bring today, and what the heart behind them truly is. Do we skim through a couple of chapters of the Bible because we need a tick on the reading plan we're working through, or do we spend time in that book because we're really expecting to hear God speak through it into our lives and situations, and want to allow space for that to happen? Do we pray because we want to tell God how much we love him, or because we have a list of needs and wants to bring to his attention? Do we give God the best part of our days, whatever that may be for you, morning or afternoon or evening? Or do we cram in a quick couple of moments when we suddenly realise we haven't truly spent any time with him at all?

Is the heart of our worship to grow in relationship with God? Or to get something out of it for ourselves? Do we come like Abel, bringing the very best of all we have to lay at his feet? Or do we come like Cain and offer something, but keep the best back for ourselves?

These are really challenging questions, and I encourage you to stop and take a moment to think about them. This, right here, is the reason Abel is at the top of the list of the heroes of faith. If you want to activate your own faith, if you want to be a person who can trust in God through anything this world or the enemy throws at you, then the first step is to check your heart. Are there areas of your life where you are holding back? Parts of your day in which you don't really want God to be involved? Are you building worship into your everyday routine, even when it comes at a cost?

> *Through Jesus, therefore, let us continually offer to God a sacrifice of praise—the fruit of lips that openly profess his name.*
>
> **-Hebrews 13:15-**

This isn't a one-time thing. This isn't something we do on a Sunday and then go about the rest of our week, putting God to one side in our busyness. We need to build this sacrifice of praise into our everyday lives. A sacrifice, by its nature, costs something, and in these tough times we all face it can be a real challenge to come and praise God. It's easier to wallow, to feel a bit miserable and sorry for yourself. It can be hard to think about the glory of God when we look at the news and see sickness and war and people hurting and broken by circumstances that are completely unfair. Praise is a sacrifice in those moments, but there is nothing like it for activating our faith all over again.

How many of the psalms begin with dread and horror and anguish, until the psalmist turns his gaze to God again, and suddenly everything is turned on its head? There may not be understanding as to why the situation hasn't changed, but there is recognition of the God who is greater than any problem we may face. As we start to praise and to worship, even through our pain, we are reminded of who our great God is, and we can't help but feel our faith activated in that remembering.

And there's more. When Abel brought his offering, when God looked at his heart and recognised Abel's pure motivation in wanting to worship the Almighty One, we're told that *God spoke well of his offerings*. God was pleased by what Abel brought. Our praise, our worship, brings a smile to the face of God.

> *The LORD delights in those who fear him, who put their hope in his unfailing love.*
>
> **-Psalm 147:11-**

Coming reverently before him in worship, recognising that he is the Creator of all, the Mighty One, the name above every other name, and a thousand other wonderful titles that do not change depending on our circumstances, recognising that causes him delight. Isn't that wonderful? God notices when you put your hope in his unfailing love. He doesn't dismiss your efforts; you're not lost in a sea of faces to him. He takes delight in you and your praises.

Worship is a good thing. It spurs us on, reminds us of God and his power and his goodness, and it activates our faith. And at the same time, it brings joy to our great Father in heaven. These are good reasons to make it a part of everyday life. We're not told that Cain and Abel brought their offerings on a particular day. It wasn't a notable celebration or special moment. On an ordinary day, Abel chose to worship, and God approved of his action. Whatever day you're reading this on, you can choose worship. You can choose to bring a sacrifice of praise to God. I don't know what that will look like for you. It might be singing, offering up a song of praise, putting on a worship track and belting along with it. It might mean a heartfelt prayer that looks beyond the things going on in your life, turning your focus back onto God. If you can't find a single word of worship to utter yourself right now, then it might mean opening up the Bible, finding a psalm and reading it out aloud, letting the praise of someone else escape from your lips.

There is always a way to praise.

We'll go on to look at characters within this list who walked by faith, acted by faith, who took great steps of faith in their lives, but right here at the start, we need to get our hearts right. We need to worship with everything, being prepared to offer all we have and all we are to God, even before he asks for it, just like Abel.

Worshipping God is the first step to activating faith.

Questions for Further Study

Background reading:
Hebrews 11:4
Genesis 4:1-8

Who were Cain and Abel? What do we know about them?

What was their experience of knowing God?

_____

_____

_____

_____

The Bible doesn't tell us why Abel's offering was acceptable and Cain's wasn't, but why do you think this was the case?

_____

_____

_____

_____

What does this tell us about how God views the offerings we bring?

_____

_____

_____

_____

Read 1 John 3:11-12.

What do these verses tell us about Cain? Why were Cain's actions evil and his brother's actions righteous?

Abel's offering was a sacrifice to him; it was the best of all he had to offer. Is there anything you would find it hard to let go of? (Your money, time, gifts, talents, etc.?) Why?

Read the following verses. What sacrifices should we be bringing as Christians?

Hebrews 13:15	
Hebrews 13:16	
Romans 12:1	
Psalm 50:14	

What is a sacrifice of praise? How do we offer it?

Why is it a sacrifice doing good to others?

Who should we be doing good to and sharing with? Are there exceptions?

What does Paul mean when he tells us to offer our bodies as living sacrifices?

Why is thanksgiving a sacrifice?

God didn't tell Cain and Abel that only meat was acceptable as an offering. In fact, later in the Bible, we read about grain offerings in Leviticus and Deuteronomy. It wasn't so much what he brought, as his motivation for bringing it.

What is your motivation for bringing the sacrifices God has asked us to bring? Do you find it easy to bring praise, to do good to others, to offer yourself as a living sacrifice and to be thankful? Are any of those sacrifices harder than others for you?

Aside from bringing an offering, Abel is also commended for something else in Hebrews 11:

And by faith Abel still speaks, even though he is dead.

What do you think this means?

Read Hebrews 12:24 and Genesis 4:10.

What does it mean when it says the sprinkled blood of Jesus speaks a better word than the blood of Abel?

Abel's life speaks to us in several different ways. He highlights the importance of bringing our own sacrifice, be it of praise, of thanksgiving, of doing good deeds, or of offering our whole lives up to God. He showcases how crucial worship is in our lives; the first example of a great person of faith we're given is of someone who brings an offering to God in worship. And finally, his death reminds us of the importance of Jesus' death. Where Abel's blood cried out for vengeance, the blood of Jesus cries out that the price for our sin has been paid.

This week, think about what you are offering to God, but more than that, think about the motivation behind it. What prompts you to pray, to read the Bible, to do good to others or go to church? Is it a desire to grow in relationship with God and bring him all the praise and glory? Or is there another motivation to do, or not do, those things?

ENOCH

THE WALK OF FAITH

Have you ever heard the expression, 'You can talk the talk but can you walk the walk?'

I grew up in a Christian household, the daughter of a pastor. When it came to faith, I knew exactly how to talk the talk. It's easy enough to sound like a wonderfully faith-filled individual when you know all the right words to say, but it can be more difficult to put those words into practice.

The next character we encounter in Hebrews 11's Hall of Faith makes Abel's story look a bit like *War and Peace*. Other than his inclusion in Hebrews 11 and a brief prophecy found in the book of Jude about the wickedness of the time he was living in, and in the times to come, Enoch's 365-year life is summed up in four verses in the book of Genesis. And yet, we know he was a man who walked the walk.

> *When Enoch had lived 65 years, he became the father of Methuselah. After he became the father of Methuselah, Enoch walked faithfully with God 300 years and had other sons and daughters. Altogether, Enoch lived a total of 365 years. Enoch walked faithfully with God; then he was no more, because God took him away.*
>
> -Genesis 5:21-24-

Enoch is one of only two people within the Bible who never experienced death, but instead were taken by God while they still lived. The other is a prophet called Elijah. He is someone we know significantly more about than Enoch. If a movie was made of the whole of the Bible's story, you can bet Elijah would have more screen time than Enoch. He was an incredible man of God, performing miracles and wonders and seeing God move in remarkable ways and even hearing the audible voice of God. His would make a great story! There, surely, was a man of faith. And yet, Elijah isn't mentioned within the list of the great heroes of faith in Hebrews 11 where this minor character, Enoch, is.

Okay, so there's something special about this man, Enoch, that's worth noting as we consider how we too can be known as people who live by faith.

> *By faith Enoch was taken from this life, so that he did not experience death: "He could not be found, because God had taken him away." For before he was taken, he was commended as one who pleased God. And without faith it is impossible to please God, because anyone who comes to him must believe that he exists and that he rewards those who earnestly seek him.*
>
> **-Hebrews 11:5-6-**

As I looked into this story I found myself asking, how good do you need to be to please God to the point that he would simply pick you up from this world and transport you straight to heaven? What incredible deeds must the saintly Enoch have done to achieve that goal? How overwhelmingly faith-filled would a person need to be to have that kind of relationship with God?

In reality though, the grand culmination of Enoch's life had nothing to do with any great deeds he had done, but rather how he had lived. As the summation of his life described in Genesis tells us, Enoch walked faithfully with God.

When this verse describes walking with God, it doesn't mean that Enoch retreated into some kind of trance-like state and wandered aimlessly through the desert, doing nothing but talking with God for the last 300 years of his life. Rather, this 'walking' is a description of his mundane, normal, day-to-day routine. We know Enoch had an everyday, normal kind of life, because we're told he had not just one, but several children, sons and daughters born during the time that Enoch walked faithfully with God. Enoch certainly wasn't a monk, cloistered away from the world, with no distractions to deter him from focussing entirely on God. He was a family man. He must have spent time providing for his wife and children, perhaps working the land or raising livestock, and all without the modern conveniences that we so often take for granted. I believe that the vast majority of Enoch's days would have been packed with activity. He had a real, normal life.

And in the midst of that normality, he walked with God. In the midst of everything he did, when he was working, relaxing, eating and drinking, playing with the kids, through it all he was walking with God.

In Romans 12:1 we're told to offer our bodies as a living sacrifice, holy and pleasing to God. We're told that this is our true and proper worship. The Message paraphrase of the Bible can help us to understand what that means:

> *So here's what I want you to do, God helping you: Take your everyday, ordinary life—your sleeping, eating, going-to-work, and walking-around life—and place it before God as an offering.*
>
> **-Romans 12:1 (MSG)-**

This links so beautifully with Abel's faith journey. His record of a faith-filled life stemmed from giving God the very best of all he had to offer, and that's exactly what Enoch was doing as well: offering his everyday, ordinary life to God.

That's something we can do too. We can choose not to compartmentalise God, leaving him in a Sunday box, or a Wednesday night Bible study box, or a mission activity box, but letting him be a part of absolutely everything we do.

Enoch's very brief story is located in the midst of a genealogy in the book of Genesis, describing the line of Adam, all the way to a man called Noah. Most of the lives of Adam's sons and grandsons and great-grandsons follow the same formula:

Enosh lived 905 years ...

Kenan lived 910 years ...

Mahalalel lived 895 years ...

They all lived their lives, but only Enoch is described as walking with God. There is a difference between walking with God in each and every day, inviting him in to each and every moment, and simply living. It's the difference between talking the talk and walking the walk.

Have you ever noticed that those days where you spend some time in the morning committing your activities to God tend to work out better than the days where you don't? It doesn't mean everything goes according to plan, it doesn't mean everything becomes easy, but in inviting God into what we're doing, we suddenly find we have the strength to cope when things don't go as we wanted them to, and the peace to accept that even if we don't understand why, God is still in control. It's only as we really learn to walk with God that we will start to see him moving in every area of our lives.

I'm still working on this. When I sit down to prepare a Bible study or a sermon I naturally come to God and pray and worship and ask him to show me what he wants me to say. And yet, in other areas of my life, in writing novels, for example, I tend to dive straight in and wonder why I'm still staring at a blank page two hours later. How much more productive would that time be if I were to bring God into it as much as I do with other things? It's all too easy to forget to invite God to be a part of what we're doing every day.

This is where Enoch's great example can encourage and inspire us again. He was a human, prone to making mistakes, to getting irritated and frustrated sometimes, and yet he managed to faithfully walk with God every day for 300 years.

That word, faithfully, is important.

Eating healthily and exercising is a battle I often find myself facing. One day, I felt a bit dispirited after letting some of the good habits I'd attempted to build into my routine slip, but I was encouraged by a note in the exercise plan I was struggling to follow. It said:

One healthy meal won't make you thin.

One unhealthy meal won't make you fat.

One day of exercising won't make you strong.

One day where you don't exercise won't make you weak. What matters is consistency.

This is true of our daily walk with God. Enoch was not a perfect man. We know that, because only Jesus was without sin. And yet, in his faithful walk, he chose to consistently return to God, over and over again. He chose to put his trust and belief in the God he had been told of from grandfather to father to son, even when it didn't make sense, even when it was hard to do, even when he'd had moments where he'd messed up.

Walking faithfully with God doesn't mean we get it right all of the time. It means we continue to come back to God when we don't, and commit, again, to inviting him into our everyday lives.

In summing up the life of Enoch, Hebrews 11 tells us:

> *Without faith it is impossible to please God, because anyone who comes to him must believe that he exists and that he rewards those who earnestly seek him.*
>
> **-Hebrews 11:6-**

Pleasing God isn't about doing a certain number of good things. It's not about being so holy that our knees bleed from all the falling on them to pray. It's not about reading the Bible so often that we can quote any Scripture and verse without a moment's hesitation. All those things are vital – prayer and Bible study and loving God's people in practical ways are things we should absolutely be doing – but without faith, you simply cannot please God, no matter what else you may try to do.

Every time we take a step of faith, every time we walk faithfully with him, every time we make a decision to live by the word and not what the world dictates, we are pleasing our God in heaven. When we earnestly seek him, devoting time to spend with him, believing that he exists, we are pleasing our God in heaven. That's the difference we find between Enoch and the other individuals in that long list in the fifth chapter of Genesis. He had grasped the concept of believing completely and utterly in the goodness of God, and seeking after him in the everyday mundanity of life. He did those things, day in and day out, until he received his incredible reward: being taken home by God, not by death.

There's a reward for us who earnestly seek after God today, as well. We have the promise of eternal life, because:

> *God so loved the world that he gave his one and only Son, that we who believe in him shall not perish, but have eternal life.*
>
> **-John 3:16-**

We have that guarantee, but we need to believe it. Perhaps the better phrase is that we need to start living as if we believe it.

We need to start walking the walk, not just talking the talk.

I love the story of Enoch, because I think we so often have an idea that to be a person of faith means doing something overwhelmingly epic with our lives. It means we should be seeing miracles every day, watching people healed as our shadow crosses them, following God's call to some remote destination, giving up every possession that we have. It can leave us feeling a bit mournful, as if our faith isn't quite as good as someone else's.

But the story of Enoch tells us that's not true. Activating our faith isn't about doing some amazing deed, being seen as some sort of super-Christian, it's simply about walking with God.

It would have been very easy to exclude Enoch from the Hebrews 11 Hall of Faith. Would any of us have noticed? It's easy enough to skim past his story, stuck as it is in the midst of a list of people who lived and died many thousands of years ago. And yet, his story was included, and there's a reason for it. When we are thinking of the first things we need to do to activate our faith, we begin with an offering, with praise and worship, as we learnt from the life of Abel, and we continue with an everyday walk of faith, as Enoch shows us. Yes, amazing and incredible and miraculous things may follow (or they may not), but these are the fundamental pillars of faith. They are the things we need to implement before anything else in our lives.

You don't need to compare your life with anyone else. Your journey of faith isn't based on outward appearances. It's an intimate walk with God, day by day.

If you're feeling that it's all a bit too late for you, that there have been too many days where you've not walked faithfully with God, then I have some good news for you from Enoch's story.

> *When Enoch had lived 65 years, he became the father of Methuselah.* ***After he became the father of Methuselah, Enoch walked faithfully with God*** *300 years and had other sons and daughters.*
>
> **-Genesis 5:21-22-**

It was only after the birth of his son, when Enoch was already sixty-five years old, that he started to walk faithfully with God. Only then did he take a belief that had perhaps only been academic and actively apply it to his life. It is never too late to start faithfully walking with God.

One day, Enoch decided he was going to change his life and let God be a part of it all with him. This could be that day for you. You can choose to let go of that one area you've been hanging on to, that one thing you haven't fully surrendered, to start walking fully and faithfully with your God.

Walk the walk, don't just talk the talk.

Questions for Further Study

Background reading:
Hebrews 11:5-6
Genesis 5:21-24

Who was Enoch?

_____
_____
_____
_____

What do the background reading passages tell you about Enoch's character?

_____
_____
_____
_____

In Hebrews 11, Enoch is commended as a man who pleased God. How can we please God?

Why is it impossible to please God without faith?

According to Hebrews 11:6, how do we get to the place of pleasing God?

Verse 6 tells us that God 'rewards those who earnestly seek him.' What does it mean to earnestly seek God?

How does God reward those who earnestly seek him?

In the account of Enoch's life in Genesis, he is described as 'walking faithfully' with God. What does walking faithfully look like?

Read Amos 3:3.
What does this verse tell you about walking with God?

What characteristics would you expect to find in the life of someone who walks with God?

How do the following verses instruct us to walk with God?

Galatians 5:16	
Ephesians 5:1-2	
Ephesians 5:8-10	
Ephesians 5:15-17	
Colossians 2:6-7	

Is there anything specific from the list above that you can apply to your life to help you to walk faithfully day by day?

Read Hebrews 12:1-2.

What hinders us from fully living our lives for God? Can you think of any examples that have prevented you from walking with him?

How can we throw off those things?

Can we walk partially with God? Or is it all or nothing?

Are there areas of your life where you're not walking faithfully with God? Think of one practical step you can take this week to invite him into that situation or area of your life.

Look at Hebrews 11:5 again:

> *By faith Enoch was taken from this life, so that he did not experience death: "He could not be found, because God had taken him away."*

Enoch's disappearance had an impact on his community. The fact that he could not be found indicates that people searched for him. His disappearance brought the focus of the people back to God.

How does our walking faithfully with God today impact our communities?

_____

_____

_____

Enoch's example shows us the importance of living a life that is walked with God. Chances are, you've had a few wobbles during the course of your life. You may be facing one right now, but the great news is that we can always start walking with him again. As we earnestly seek him out, we will find him. And as we remember the amazing reward we have coming, along with the wonderful benefits of walking with him here on earth, we have an incredible incentive to seek him out and take every step faithfully with him.

NOAH
FAITH IN ACTION

There are some great 'buts' in the Bible.

> *For the wages of sin is death, but the gift of God is eternal life in Christ Jesus our Lord..*
>
> **-Romans 6:23-**
>
> *My flesh and my heart may fail, but God is the strength of my heart and my portion forever.*
>
> **-Psalm 73:26-**
>
> *The LORD saw how great the wickedness of the human race had become on the earth, and that every inclination of the thoughts of the human heart was only evil all the time ... **But Noah found favour in the eyes of the LORD**.*
>
> **-Genesis 6:5,8-**

It's amazing how often that tiny word can turn the whole story around. We are completely undeserving of salvation, but God, with his infinite store of mercy and grace, gifts it to us. We may feel weak and overwhelmed, but God is our strength forever, every day of our lives. And in a time of the world when evil flourished in every heart and mind, one man stood out for something different.

That man was called Noah.

I think it's fair to say that we know a bit more about this particular character than the first two offerings in Hebrews 11's Hall of Faith. Noah's story always takes me back to my Sunday School days. If you choose not to emphasise the mass death and destruction, it makes a great story for children: a giant boat, animals strolling in two by two, a big rainstorm and a merry little cruise for Noah and his family for a few nights.

In reality though, there is far more to this story. It's the tale of a man who faced ridicule to follow God's instruction, a man who spent decades of his life creating something that must have seemed utterly ludicrous, and a man who went on to watch as his neighbours, his friends, died in an enormous flood which was beyond the comprehension of anyone who lived on earth. Noah may have known it was coming, but it must still have been an incredibly traumatic time for the family, who had to spend over a year in an enclosed space, enjoying only each other's company as they tended to the animals aboard and wondered if they would ever set foot on dry ground again. I don't care how perfect your family dynamic may be, that would be a trying time for any of us!

It's a fairly harrowing story when you really start to think about it, and one which can certainly teach us lessons about faith, as we discover in Hebrews 11.

> *By faith Noah, when warned about things not yet seen, in holy fear built an ark to save his family. By his faith he condemned the world and became heir of the righteousness that is in keeping with faith.*
>
> **-Hebrews 11:7-**

It feels like the perfect definition of faith. Noah was asked, by God, to undertake a great task, one that would be difficult, one that would be a sacrifice, and he did it. How did Noah get to this point? How was his faith so very strong that he was happy to undertake a project that would have seemed so utterly ridiculous, with no physical evidence whatsoever of what God had warned him about? I find it hard enough to motivate myself to sit by my computer and write these words some days; how much harder it would have been for Noah to take on a task so far beyond reason as to make no sense whatsoever in this world.

We'll get to that ark-building moment of madness, but it's important to consider Noah's life before God dropped that bombshell into it. The Bible tells us that:

> *Noah was a righteous man, blameless among the people of his time, and he walked faithfully with God.*
>
> **-Genesis 6:9-**

That's a bit different to the description of the rest of humanity that we read earlier, with every inclination of the thoughts of the human heart only evil, all of the time.

> *Now God saw that the earth had become corrupt and was filled with violence. God observed all this corruption in the world, for everyone on earth was corrupt.*
>
> **-Genesis 6:11-12 (NLT)-**

Violence and corruption were the rule of the day. They filled the heart of every human on earth.

The human race can be pretty atrocious today. You only need to look at the news to see the evil and wickedness that exists in societies around the globe, but occasionally there are good deeds that stand out. Those moments where people say, 'it restores your faith in humanity,' when someone rescues a cat from a tree or makes a sacrificial gesture to help a stranger. In the days of Noah, those moments didn't exist. The thoughts of the human heart were only evil, all the time. In that world, faced with that level of wickedness, Noah was named a righteous man, blameless among the people he dwelt with. He was not without sin, he was still human, still made mistakes, but he was still notably righteous among the rest of the people living in the world.

This is even more remarkable when you consider that:

> *Noah was six hundred years old when the floodwaters came on the earth.*
>
> **-Genesis 7:6-**

In the midst of all of that wickedness and violence and corruption, Noah had remained faithful to God for 600 years. He was faithful in living his life every day.

If you take the ark out of the equation, Noah's story sounds remarkably similar to that of Enoch, whom we considered in the last chapter. Noah walked faithfully with God for hundreds of years before he knew that God planned to wipe away mankind in a flood. He didn't choose faithfulness because it was the only option to save himself and his family; he lived a faithful life, every day, because he knew the Lord and saw that following after him was a better way of living than what the rest of the world had chosen.

Noah is, and always will be, remembered for his incredible faith in action, following God's instruction to build an ark. I'm not disparaging that at all. It was a huge undertaking and a massive step of faith, but sometimes I wonder whether living for 600 years, completely surrounded by wickedness and sin, and not giving into it, wasn't a bigger step of faith. There were probably millions of small steps of faith in reality, echoing the teaching of Jesus.

> *If you are faithful in little things, you will be faithful in large ones.*
> **-Luke 16:10 (NLT)-**

I imagine there were moments in Noah's 600 years of life where he doubted. The entire population had forgotten and forsaken their God. Only he and his family held out. Did he perhaps wonder if he was wrong, and the rest of the world had the right idea?

Have you perhaps wondered the same? Have you ever experienced a moment of doubt where your faith has wavered, shrinking in the face of a world that has, again, forgotten its Saviour?

Stay strong!

Through each moment, in each day, your faith is being developed to allow you to face the next big challenge. You may not be called to gather a load of wood from your local DIY store to start building an ark, but there will be times in your life where you will need to hold tightly to the truth you know. When you can stick to God through every doubt that may plague your mind, you will be ready for the challenge when it hits. You will be ready to put your faith into action. Your everyday, little faithfulness is preparing you for that moment when you, just like Noah, may need to trust for something unseen, something bigger, a mountain that seems truly immovable, that needs the activated faith you are developing in the normal, everyday mundanity of life.

I imagine it was a fairly normal day when Noah's life abruptly changed, when God called him to take a big step, a giant leap really, of faith. I can picture Noah desperately searching for something to write the instructions down with, "Wait just a moment, God. Shem, fetch me a pen!"

Those giant, faith-stretching moments can come at any time.

I found myself in a conference at my local church when the speaker told us to write down the dreams that had been lying dormant in our hearts, and in separate parts of the room, both myself and my husband Dave inked down the word 'mission.' Life had been fairly normal until that moment. Dave had a good job, and I was volunteering part-time at our church, with a growing ministry preaching in churches in the surrounding area. The call came, and life as we knew it was about to change. Within a year we found ourselves living in Africa.

You never know when God will whisper into your normal, everyday life, telling you it's time to build your ark, to step out of your comfortable boat to walk on the water. It's terrifying, but it's exhilarating, and when you look back on your life, you'll see that God was preparing you for the big step, through every small step of faithfulness on your journey.

Noah's ark was an enormous undertaking. It was a huge structure to build. I don't know exactly how Noah spent his free time before the call; some farming, a bit of carpentry perhaps, he may well have built his own home, but this was another level entirely. He would need to learn new skills, to expend considerable resources, and he would have to undertake a task that would have been exceedingly dangerous, manoeuvring heavy pieces of wood, just him and his sons. In the meantime, his family would still have needed food and other provisions to survive that building time.

Bible scholars are divided on how long the construction of the ark may have taken, but estimates seem to range from forty years up to 100. This was not a one-week undertaking. This was decades of Noah's life. How much more powerful this little verse becomes when we consider those timescales:

> *Noah did everything just as God commanded him.*
> **-Genesis 6:22-**

We don't know if God spoke to Noah at all again in the time between the giving of the instructions and the moment the rain began to fall, and yet Noah continued to do everything that God had commanded him, day in and day out, for decades.

And those instructions were good. Modern tankers and freight-hauling ships sailing the seas today are built to the same 6:1 ratio Noah was given by God. It turns out, a ship six times as long as it is wide is the most stable design for a seacraft that we have been able to come up with. The design of Noah's ark allowed for 20,000 tons of cargo to be carried. No bigger ship would be built until the 1800s. God knew exactly what he was doing in the instructions he gave to Noah, but Noah didn't know that.

How often do we find ourselves in the same situation? God gives us an instruction which seems completely crazy on the surface. You want me to do what, God? You want me to move to Africa? You want me to leave behind friends and family and everything that I've ever known? Do you realise, God, that to do what you're asking, I will need to raise tens of thousands of pounds of financial support every single year? How am I supposed to do that?

Those were certainly questions in my head after that out-of-the-blue call to step into the unknown of this missionary lifestyle. And yet, several years in, I can look back and see God's faithfulness at work in every step. Our small steps of faith are met by God's incalculable faithfulness. His master plan is immense and unstoppable and incredible, and he invites us to be a part of it, our faith in action meeting his wonderful provision and glory and grace. There is nothing more exciting than stepping into the unknown, than following the instruction, and seeing God on the move.

If God is asking you to take action, it doesn't matter how big or small the action is. You don't need to compare your life with anyone else's. This is between you and God. You may find yourself asking those similar questions. How am I supposed to have a conversation with that person who clearly has no interest in God? How am I supposed to found that ministry? How am I supposed to find my place in this new school or workplace? How am I supposed to raise godly children in a world that, as in Noah's time, is becoming increasingly more wicked?

It's okay to ask those questions. It's okay to have those moments of doubt. You've not failed if that's where you find yourself right now. The Bible is littered with characters who had those same moments, and who still went on to see God work in incredible ways. We may not know the eventual outcome of what God is asking us to do, may not have all the details, but we can trust in God's master plan. We can trust that he has worked out all of the practicalities, even if we don't need to know them right now. All we need to do is take that step, follow that instruction, do what he is asking us to do, and:

> *Trust in the LORD with all your heart and lean not on your own understanding; in all your ways submit to him, and he will make your paths straight.*
>
> **-Proverbs 3:5-6-**

Could we become a people who, like Noah, trust in the Lord with all our hearts, following after him and simply getting on with it when God sets a path before us? I would like to think so, though I know it won't be an easy task. Building an ark certainly wasn't.

Whether or not you're facing an ark-building moment right now, or simply facing down another year of life, you need to live faithfully, to be ready for that next big step, to be faithful in the small and big things. We need to respond like Noah and say, okay God, I might not understand exactly how this is going to work, but I'm going to trust in you and do what you say, this day and every day for the rest of my life.

Activated faith is faith in action.

Questions for Further Study

Background reading:
Hebrews 11:7
Genesis 6:1 – 9:17

The background reading for the story of Noah is quite long, but I encourage you to read it. Try to put yourself in the midst of the story; imagine how Noah and the people around him would have felt and what it would have been like building something that had never been built before, to protect your family from something that had never been experienced before.

Who was Noah?

Does anything stand out to you from his story? If so what, and why?

Consider Hebrews 11:7 again:

By faith Noah, when warned about things not yet seen, in holy fear built an ark to save his family. By his faith he condemned the world and became heir of the righteousness that is in keeping with faith.

What does it mean that Noah acted with 'holy fear', or with reverence, as he built the ark?

_____
_____
_____
_____

Is holy fear, or reverence, necessary for obedience?

_____
_____
_____
_____

How can we show God reverence? What does it mean for us to act in holy fear?

_____
_____
_____
_____

What was Noah's reward for his faithfulness?

In Genesis 6:9 we are told Noah was a righteous man, and yet Hebrews 11:7 tells us he became heir of the righteousness that is in keeping with faith, because of his action. **What do these verses tell us about being righteous?**

Are we rewarded for acting in faith today? If so, how?

Read John 14:15, John 14:23-24 and James 1:22.
What do these verses tell us about obeying God?

What questions run through your mind when God asks you to step out in obedience? How do you respond?

Genesis 6:22 tells us that:

Noah did everything just as God commanded him.

How would you rate your own level of obedience to Jesus?

How could it be improved?

Obeying God can be difficult when it seems the whole world is against you. Noah almost certainly faced ridicule for building his ark, just as Jesus and Paul were accused of being mad for their teaching. See John 10:20 and Acts 26:24.

How can we obey the voice of God when it seems contrary to human reason?

Read Matthew 24:36-39.

How does this passage compare the time of the coming of Christ with Noah's time?

What does that mean for us today?

Read 2 Timothy 3:1-5.

How does today's moral climate compare to Noah's time, and to the time Paul speaks about as related to the last days?

How does the moral climate of the world impact you?

_____

_____

_____

Noah was not a perfect man; only Jesus was perfect and without sin. And yet, in a time of great wickedness, he resolved to listen to the voice of God over the other voices shouting for his attention. He chose to be obedient to God's command and didn't waver, even though the decision cost him financially and caused him to be a laughingstock, so he was recorded as a man of faith. What a great example and a challenge to us today, to be people who stand for God,

ABRAHAM

FAITH IN THE UNKNOWN

"I don't know what it is about that country, but I'm sure we're going to end up there," said my husband, Dave, after his first trip to the tiny west African nation of Liberia. He'd spent a week there, leaving our comfortable and familiar home in Uganda to install some electrical equipment into one of Mission Aviation Fellowship's planes in Liberia's capital city of Monrovia.

If you say so, I thought to myself.

And yet, as time went by, as Dave returned again to Liberia and again felt the tug of his heartstrings, we realised God was preparing us for another move. We were called into the unknown again. It would mean leaving behind friends, again, learning a new culture, again, surrendering the country of Uganda which had become dear to our hearts into God's hands.

Stepping into the unknown would be difficult.

But is anything really unknown these days? Even after Dave's first mention of Liberia I found myself delving into all Google had to say about this new and very different country. I could look at detailed maps showing where we would live, satellite imagery of what it looked like in great detail. I could look up video documentaries on YouTube, giving me a glimpse of the country's turbulent history. I could contact individuals living in

Monrovia through Facebook and WhatsApp. There has never been a time when we have had so much information at our fingertips, and though it didn't answer all my questions about Liberia, it gave me a good idea what I would be walking into.

The next character in our investigation of faith did not have that luxury.

> *By faith Abraham, when called to go to a place he would later receive as his inheritance, obeyed and went, even though he did not know where he was going.*
>
> **-Hebrews 11:8-**

Abraham is one of the most mentioned characters in the Bible. His story spans from Genesis chapter 11, all the way through to his death in chapter 25. He is spoken of in numerous Old and New Testament books, painted as the father of faith throughout them all. Condensing his life into a few pages is impossible, but we can consider those specific moments that the Hall of Faith calls our attention to. This was a man prepared to leave everything that he knew, to move to a completely unknown destination.

We don't know too much about Abraham as a young man. His name was Abram in those days, and he had a father called Terah, a couple of brothers, one of whom sadly died, a nephew called Lot and a barren wife, Sarai. The entire family leaves the country where Abram and his brothers were born, Ur of the Chaldeans (or Mesopotamia, to give it its other name), heading for Canaan.

> *The God of glory appeared to our father Abraham while he was still in Mesopotamia, before he lived in Harran. 'Leave your country and your people,' God said, 'and go to the land I will show you.'*
>
> -Acts 7:2-3-

A call from God started the family moving, and yet, when they reached a place called Harran along the way, they stopped and settled.

Pause for a moment here and consider this. The father of faith himself stopped partway through an instruction given to him specifically by God. We don't know exactly how long he lived in Harran, but long enough for them to have settled in and, eventually, for Terah to die there. Perhaps it was comfortable there. Perhaps Terah and Abram's brother, Nahor, had no desire to move on any further. Perhaps Abram was reluctant to continue on his own, knowing his wife was not able to conceive, knowing his wealth and belongings would at least stay in the family if he remained with them.

This doesn't exactly sound like the hero of faith we've come to know.

What a reassurance that is for us! Abraham's record in Hebrews 11 doesn't say, by faith Abraham, when called to go to a place he would later receive as his inheritance, eventually obeyed and went, after giving up partway through the first time and needing to be reminded by God again to get moving. Isn't it wonderful that our faith isn't tarnished by the times we get it wrong? There's no record here of any delay, of any hesitation, of any giving in to comfort. Why? Because Abraham did, eventually, get moving. He did follow that command reiterated in Genesis 12:1:

> *The LORD had said to Abram, "Go from your country, your people and your father's household to the land I will show you."*
>
> **-Genesis 12:1-**

If God has given you a specific instruction and you've been dragging your heels about following it, that's okay. It's not too late. Abram was seventy-five years of age when God reawakened his call. This is after the time when we hear of people living for numerous centuries; Abraham lived to be 175. More years than we can expect, maybe, but he was still a good way through his life when he decided it was time to get going again. It's never too late for God to give you a new call, or to reawaken an old one. It's never too late for you to act on it.

We don't actually know if God spoke to Abram again in Harran, or whether Abram simply remembered the call he'd received in the land of Ur after the death of his father, but something kickstarted his journey again, and this time, he was happy to follow the instruction completely, to leave his people, his father's household, and to step into the unknown.

Hebrews 12:2 tells us that God is both the *pioneer* and the *perfecter of faith*. He is the pioneer, the catalyst that starts us believing, the God who whispered to an unknown man living in a pagan nation that all peoples on earth would one day be blessed through him. God is also the perfecter of faith, taking that little morsel we have and stretching it, forgiving us mercifully when we make mistakes, but continuing to push us gently into our purpose, reminding Abram that it was time to move on.

I always enjoy the humanity of the characters we encounter in the Bible. Abram was not perfect, and nor was his faith, but through God's pioneering and perfecting work, his faith is something we can look back on and be encouraged by. Your faith doesn't need to be perfect, but you do need to be open to God's perfecting process. You don't need to get there on your own.

Let's consider this journey that Abram made.

Go from your people and your father's household, God told him. Leave behind friends and family, with no Skype or Zoom for a quick call, not even a postal service. You may never see them again. That's a big deal. Leave behind your relatives, those you should be helping to support, leave behind your responsibilities to them, leave behind the closeness and familiarity of those relationships.

Go to the land I will show you, God told him. No map, no foreign office website telling you the potential risks of the place you're going to, not even the name of a town or city that could be your final destination. Abram had never been to Canaan; he had no idea what the culture may be like, what gods they may worship, whether the natives would be welcoming or hostile. He didn't know whether there would be sufficient food or water on the way for his household.

If it was me, I think I would have asked God for a bit more information. 'Perhaps you could let me know where I'm going before I set out, then you wouldn't have to show me on the way.' We want all the information at the outset for any journeys we may undertake, be they real physical travels or metaphorical movements in our lives.

We all face journeys into the unknown. They may not be as dramatic as walking off in a direction with all of our belongings packed onto camels, but that doesn't mean they are any less significant. We face journeys into new jobs or new relationships or new ministries, journeys in overcoming problems or sins in our lives that we struggle to shake, journeys in growing in our relationships with God. We don't ever stop travelling in our lives, and as much as we would love to know the final destination and all the details for the road ahead, we don't normally get them. In my experience, God has tended to guide me one step at a time, revealing only what I need to know for that next movement.

> *So Abram went, as the LORD had told him.*
> **-Genesis 12:4a-**

Despite the uncertainties and the unknowns, Abram went. God called, and he answered. Without knowing what was ahead, and leaving behind what he knew and loved dearly, he left.

At some point in his time in Harran, Abram came to the realisation that what may be unknown to him is absolutely not unknown to God. We may not be able to see the outcome of a situation, but we can rest in the assurance that God can. This is a life-changing truth, if we can grasp hold of it. What a relief it is that we don't need to know everything, that we can trust that God will lead us where we need to go, that he will make the path clear as we tread on it.

In order to take that first step though, we need to be open to hearing from God.

> *Jesus Christ is the same yesterday and today and forever.*
> **-Hebrews 13:8-**

If we genuinely believe that God is unchanging, that he is the same yesterday as he is today as he will be tomorrow, then we should believe that God is ready and willing to speak to us, to offer us guidance for whatever journey we may face, just as he did for Abram all those years ago. The question is: how much time do we take out of our busy days and weeks and months and years to listen to what he might have to say to us? Would Abram have heard that wonderful word from God, *I will make you into a great nation, and I will bless you*, if he had been distracted by his smartphone? I can't count the number of times I have sat down to pray and been disturbed by that little beep I know I should ignore. But, once the thought of it is in my head, there's no dismissing it.

We live in a connected world full of unending distraction. We live in a world that is incredibly self-focussed, in the search for our best lives, for everything that will be good for me. Those cultural influences can infiltrate our prayer lives, leaving our precious moments with God more like recounting a shopping list of things we think we need. It's not bad to bring those things to God, but we should always remember that our Father knows what we need before we ask him.[3] God is still speaking to us today, but are we making the time to listen?

I doubt that the road to Canaan was a perfect straight line with no deviations to the right or left. As Abram and Sarai and Lot travelled into the distance, Abram must have stayed receptive along the way, waiting for God's gentle leading to bring him to the right place. It can be all too easy for us to get swept up in doing something new which God has dropped into our hearts. We can get so passionate about seeing things through according to how we think they should go that we can get off course, wandering on a tangent that takes us to a different outcome. It's so important to stay receptive to God, even on the journey.

> *Abram travelled through the land as far as the site of the great tree of Moreh at Shechem. At that time the Canaanites were in the land. The LORD appeared to Abram and said, "To your offspring I will give this land." So he built an altar there to the LORD, who had appeared to him.*
>
> **-Genesis 12:6-7-**

God didn't abandon Abram on the way. Instead, he reiterated his promise once Abram arrived, letting him know he was in the right place. God won't simply start you off and then leave you to it; he's with you in every single step you take. Remember, he is the pioneer and the perfecter, the God who starts you off on the journey, and the God who walks with you through the muck and the mire, through the mountaintops and the valleys. Whether you're completely on the right track in your life, or in a place where you need to realign yourself with his original promise and purpose, it's imperative that you stay receptive and open to his word.

Life wasn't easy for Abram, even when he reached the place of promise. He faced famine and made mistakes. You can read all about his story in the book of Genesis. It's a fascinating tale, but through it all, even after those moments where he wavered, he held to God's promise, and to his faith.

> *By faith he made his home in the promised land like a stranger in a foreign country; he lived in tents, as did Isaac and Jacob, who were heirs with him of the same promise. For he was looking forward to the city with foundations, whose architect and builder is God.*
>
> **-Hebrews 11:9-10-**

Abram did not live to see all peoples on earth blessed through him. He didn't live to see descendants as numerous as the stars in the sky. He lived as a stranger, as a foreigner, never quite belonging. It was only through faith that he could hold out hope for the promise he would never see fulfilled. After taking one big step of faith, it can be easy for us to think that we've done our bit, we've reached the end, we're going to start seeing God's promises fulfilled left, right and centre, but then nothing seems to happen and we're left feeling discouraged. If you're in that place today, hold on to those promises.

> *Let us hold unswervingly to the hope we profess, for he who promised is faithful.*
>
> **-Hebrews 10:23-**

Your faithful Father has not forgotten his promises to you.

Abram, later Abraham, had his perspective right. He was looking forwards, not backwards, thinking eternally, not presently. We can do the same. We are foreigners in this world; our home is in heaven. Holding to that truth can activate our faith, even when circumstances work out in ways we don't expect. We may never see the end result of the paths we're walking on now, but that doesn't mean God isn't working through us. Something incredible can and will be birthed through your walk of faith, regardless of whether you see the outcome.

Stepping out on a new journey, any new journey, can be difficult, but by trusting in Almighty God, listening to his direction, staying receptive to new instructions and keeping his promises alive in our hearts, we can see our promised land, just as Abraham did, and we can keep our hopes set on the heavenly country we will one day inherit.

> *All these people were still living by faith when they died. They did not receive the things promised; they only saw them and welcomed them from a distance, admitting that they were foreigners and strangers on earth. People who say such things show that they are looking for a country of their own. If they had been thinking of the country they had left, they would have had opportunity to return. Instead, they were longing for a better country—a heavenly one. Therefore God is not ashamed to be called their God, for he has prepared a city for them.*
>
> -Hebrews 11:13-16-

Questions for Further Study

Background reading:

Hebrews 11:8-10

Genesis 11:27 – 12:9

Abraham's story in the Bible spans fourteen chapters of Genesis, and he features regularly in other books in the Old and New Testament as well. It would be impossible to look into all of this information, so we will explore a few different parts of his life in the coming chapters.

Who was Abram? What do we know about him and his family?

Read Hebrews 11:8.

What did God ask Abraham to do? What was Abraham's response?

How do you know when God is leading you to do something?

Do you find it easy to obey when God asks you to step out of your comfort zone?

What does God promise concerning the path he has for us in the following verses?

Psalm 32:8	
Psalm 37:23-24	
Proverbs 16:9	
Proverbs 20:24	

Did any of these verses resound with you? Why?

Read Acts 7:2-3 and Genesis 11:31.

When did God first speak to Abraham about leaving for the Promised Land?

What happened after the family set out on their journey? Why do you think this happened?

How can we stop ourselves settling part way to the promise?

Hebrews 11:9 goes on to tell us that, "By faith he [Abraham] made his home in the promised land like a stranger in a foreign country."

Read Genesis 12:10-20.

It wasn't plain sailing for Abraham after he arrived at his destination. What did he do when faced with a famine?

What insights do you gain about Abraham based on the situation in Egypt?

Despite hearing from God on several occasions and seeing God come through for him on the journey, bringing him safely to the land of promise, Abraham's faith still wavered when he reached his destination.

If God is true to his word when he makes a promise, why do we doubt?

How can we keep our own faith from wavering?

Read Genesis 13:1-2.

Despite Abraham's wobble in faith during his trip to Egypt, he left there a wealthy man. What does this tell us about God's character?

Read Hebrews 11:9-10.

What was Abraham looking forward to?

What do you find yourself looking forward to? Do you find it easy or difficult to keep an eternal mindset in day-to-day life?

Despite a road that was rocky at times, Abraham is described as the father of faith in the Bible. Galatians 3:7 tells us that *those who have faith are children of Abraham*. Despite his mistakes, he was still a hero of faith. What an encouragement to us today. If you find your faith wavering, you can get back on track, get out of your metaphorical Egypt, and back to your place of promise. It's never too late to start walking on the path God has in store for you.

SARAH

FAITH THROUGH THE WAIT

Waiting.

Why must so many Bible stories involve waiting? There was a thirteen-year gap between Joseph's dreams and his becoming the Egyptian prime minister; thirteen years of slavery and imprisonment. The teenage David, anointed to be king of the nation of Israel, wouldn't see the throne for a good fifteen years or so, the last few years of which he spent fleeing for his life, living in caves. And Sarah, the wife of Abraham, our next character in this exploration of faith, had to wait twenty-five years from the first promise of descendants as numerous as the stars until the first cries of her baby boy, Isaac.

I believe that in this point in history, perhaps more than any other, we are an impatient people. We live in a world of instant, of fast food and next-day (or even same day) delivery, of any piece of information you could ever want at your fingertips, of television shows and movies available at the push of a button.

Waiting is not something we're used to.

And yet, waiting is often something we need to do. It's in the wait that we learn to recognise God's perfect timing and plan. It's in the wait that we realise we simply can't do it alone. It's in the wait that our faith is pushed to the limit, and after successful waiting, is activated to believe that anything, absolutely anything, is possible with God.

Without the wait, we wouldn't need to learn those essential truths, but while the wait might be beneficial, it's certainly not comfortable.

The pages of the Bible are filled with tales of waiting, from Daniel, fasting and praying for twenty-one days for an answer to his prayers, to Lazarus, dead in the grave for a full four days. From the lame man who sat at the temple gate called Beautiful all of his life, who must have heard, potentially even seen, Jesus walk by and yet remained unhealed, until the moment that Peter and John prayed for him, to an old man called Simeon, who waited, day in and day out at the temple to see the promised Messiah, having been told he would not die before that moment.

Over and over, we see people waiting: waiting to hear God speak, waiting to see God act. I find it hard enough to sit and wait for five minutes in a prayer time to listen for God's guidance; there's always something to distract me – thoughts for the day ahead or the incessant beeping of my phone. If I feel God telling me something is going to happen, I expect it to happen right away. I don't want to have to wait years for it. And yet, in my experience, it's the things that are impossible – the tallest mountains, the biggest miracles –that require the longest wait, and those things are always worth it.

God's timing is perfect, but it can be difficult to remember that in a season of waiting.

That's a lesson we certainly learn from the life of Sarah.

> *Abram and Nahor both married. The name of Abram's wife was Sarai… Now Sarai was childless because she was not able to conceive.*
>
> **-Genesis 11:29-30-**

This is our first introduction to the character of Sarah (then Sarai) in the Bible. From the outset, we know this woman is barren, unable to have children. I can imagine how her heart must have leapt when Abraham first received the promise that he was to become a great nation. 'God's going to heal me,' she must have thought. 'I'm going to have children after all.' But then the days and the weeks and the months and the years pass by, and month by month, she feels the disappointment as, once again, she fails to conceive until, eventually, it's too late.

It's at that point that Sarah takes matters into her own hands. She offers her Egyptian slave girl, Hagar, to her husband, hoping to bear a child that way. Now at the time, this was a legitimate option. A servant could be given to the husband, and children born in that manner would count as belonging to the wife. We see the same concept with Jacob's wives later in the book of Genesis, as the sisters Leah and Rachel compete to give Jacob the most sons, and offer their servants to add to their own count.

According to human logic, therefore, Sarah's solution was perfect. It answered all their problems. With the benefit of hindsight, however, we see that it was anything but. The birth of Ishmael caused rifts within the family, and to this day we see the fallout of the decision, as the Arabic people, born through the line of Ishmael, war against the Jewish nation, born through the line of Isaac.

At the time, though, it must have seemed like Sarah's only option. I can't begin to imagine her heartache day after day, feeling that she was letting down her husband, on whom the promise of numerous descendants lay, not to mention the feeling of incompleteness she must have nursed, in a culture where having children to continue the family was incredibly important. Did she feel like a failure? Did she wonder if she had done something wrong?

Perhaps you've asked yourself similar questions through a time of waiting.

Perhaps, like Sarah, you've considered ways to make something happen that seems to have stalled, even if you know, deep down, those methods are not right.

After the birth of Ishmael, Abraham was visited by some angelic guests who had a startling proclamation to make:

> *Then one of them said, "I will surely return to you about this time next year, and Sarah your wife will have a son."*
>
> *Now Sarah was listening at the entrance to the tent, which was behind him. Abraham and Sarah were already very old, and Sarah was past the age of childbearing. So Sarah laughed to herself as she thought, "After I am worn out and my lord is old, will I now have this pleasure?"*
>
> **-Genesis 18:10-12-**

Consider that at this point, Abraham was 100 years old. Sarah herself was over ninety. Sarah laughed. I don't blame her. I think I'd have laughed too. But more than that, when the Lord calls her on her laughter, she lies about it.

> *Then the LORD said to Abraham, "Why did Sarah laugh and say, 'Will I really have a child, now that I am old?' Is anything too hard for the LORD? I will return to you at the appointed time next year, and Sarah will have a son."*
>
> *Sarah was afraid, so she lied and said, "I did not laugh."*
>
> *But he said, "Yes, you did laugh."*
>
> **-Genesis 18:13-15-**

In her moment of terror and doubt, she brazenly lies to two angels and the Lord himself. She fakes the faith, not wanting to admit that she does consider this particular request to be a bit too hard for God. How often do we pretend that we believe in a promise, I wonder, faking it in our churches, in our marriages, even to God himself, when really, we simply want to burst out laughing at the absurdity of it all? When really, we're doubting that such an impossible thing could ever come to pass.

This is the woman listed in Hebrews 11 as a hero of faith. A woman who failed to trust that God would miraculously fulfil his promise, and instead tried to orchestrate the miracle herself. A woman who laughed behind God's back at the thought she could possibly see her heart's desire fulfilled.

> *And by faith even Sarah, who was past childbearing age, was enabled to bear children because she considered him faithful who had made the promise. And so from this one man, and he as good as dead, came descendants as numerous as the stars in the sky and as countless as the sand on the seashore.*
>
> **-Hebrews 11:11-12-**

Isn't this the most beautiful testimony of God's incredible mercy and grace? The record in the book of Hebrews doesn't say, 'Sarah, who messed up multiple times so that God eventually took pity on her.' No. It says, 'Sarah, who considered him faithful.'

Be encouraged today. No matter how many mistakes you might have made, trying to do things in your own strength and your own way, no matter how many times you might have laughed to yourself at the possibility of God's promise coming true, it's not too late. In turning back to God, in recognising who he is, you can reactivate your faith again. You can be a person known, not for being plagued by doubts, but for believing the promise, no matter what may have happened in the past.

In Sarah's journey to activating her faith, she learnt that nothing is impossible for God. Hebrews 11 tells us that she was past childbearing age. There are no ifs, buts or maybes here; if you asked any doctor, they would tell you it was impossible for this woman to have children. It's easy to skim past verses like this in the Bible and fail to recognise their significance. Sarah having a child was not a long shot; there was no way on earth it could ever happen, until God entered the scene.

The Israelites were trapped against the Red Sea. There was literally no means of escape for them. Until God entered the scene. Three Israelite men, captured and taken to Babylon, found themselves thrown into a fiery furnace. They should have died. But God entered the scene. A young man faced down a giant trained in warfare, and singlehandedly brought him down with a single stone. It was impossible, shouldn't have happened, but God entered the scene.

The wonderful news for us today is that, regardless of what the world tells us is impossible, we have the knowledge that nothing is impossible for God. He is master of the impossible, and when he enters the scene, there is nothing he cannot do.

That's easy to say, of course. It's harder to believe when you find yourself clinging on to a promise when everyone around you is screaming that it can't be done, and even your own traitorous mind tends to agree. That's when looking at an example like Sarah's can be such an encouragement to us today. She started by laughing at what the world told her was impossible, but through a reactivation of faith, hearing the Lord speak the promise again, she was able to overcome her disbelief, and so learnt the lesson that nothing is impossible for God.

I love the way the Hebrews account phrases Sarah's (eventual) belief:

> *And by faith even Sarah, who was past childbearing age, was enabled to bear children because she considered him faithful who had made the promise.*
>
> **-Hebrews 11:11-**

She knew who had made the promise. She knew where the promised blessing had come from and that was something she could hold on to, even in the midst of her doubts. I don't think it's a coincidence that when the angelic visitors popped over for a nice barbecue with Abraham, that they spoke to him in the hearing of Sarah. In previous moments, we've only heard of God speaking directly to Abraham, and yet, this time, she hears for herself. When you spot the LORD in capital letters in your Bible in the Old Testament, it's referring to the distinctive, personal name of the God of Israel, Yahweh, or Jehovah, as it's been translated into our English Bibles. Sarah heard the Lord speak for herself. She suddenly had an increased awareness of the one who had made the promise.

When the entire world is determined to flatten your dream, and the enemy is throwing everything he can at you to stop you achieving what God has told you that you can do, that's when you need to remember who made the promise. What a wonder it is today that we have access to the Bible, that we can pick up the word of God at any time, day or night, and remind ourselves of all God says about who he is, and about who we are. Do that, when the doubts creep in. Do that, when the wait grinds on and you feel frustrated. Remember who made the promise.

But, more than that, remember the character of the one who made the promise. Sarah considered him faithful. She stopped, she thought about it, and her considered conclusion was that God is faithful. Look back on your life. Has there ever been a moment when God's faithfulness has lacked? Has there ever been a moment when he has left you? He is so very faithful, and that can inspire faith to rise in us, to be reactivated in us. The faithful God is worth putting our faith in.

> *If we are faithless, he remains faithful, for he cannot disown himself.*
>
> **-2 Timothy 2:13-**

No matter how faithless we might have been in the past, he remains faithful. Stop and consider that faithfulness when the wait drains you and you wonder if God even cares, if he's even with you any longer. He will never leave you, will never forsake you. He is eternally faithful.

Perhaps you've heard the expression, 'God will never give you more than you can handle.' Sadly, it's not true. We will consistently face situations that seem impossible in our lives, mountains that seem utterly immovable. Sarah and Abraham could not possibly have had a child on their own, and yet God enabled her to become the mother of a nation that would change the world. She became an ancestor of Jesus. If the task before you seems to be too big for you, that's okay; trust in God's faithfulness, stay the course, and he will provide you with the strength you need. His dreams are even bigger than our own, and he has the power to bring them all to pass.

When we get to grips with this idea, it's even possible for us to enjoy the waiting time. When we recognise that God has our best interests at heart, and trust that he knows what he's doing, then we can quiet the restlessness of our hearts, and tune in to him again. It will stop us trying to make things happen ourselves, in ways that are not helpful, and will help us to stay connected, to grow closer to God, even in our desperation to see his promise fulfilled.

It is possible to wait well, but only when we stay connected to God.

Perhaps there is something you have been called to birth: a new ministry, a business, a new way of doing day-to-day life which glorifies him, an opportunity to reach the lost. If you find yourself in that place, it's all too easy to feel defeated before you even begin, to laugh and question how it could ever come about.

Remember Sarah. Allow your faith to be activated again, just as hers was, by looking to our Lord and Saviour, Christ Jesus, who is capable of working in us and through us to do even the most impossible tasks.

And if you need to wait for a while, wait well, trusting in God's perfect timing. Let your faith awaken, as you look forward to the moment when he will move.

Questions for Further Study

Background reading:

Hebrews 11:11-12
Genesis 16
Genesis 18:1-15
Genesis 21:1-7

In some translations of the Bible, the Hebrews 11 passage focuses more on Abraham than Sarah. This is how it reads in the NIV:

> *And by faith even Sarah, who was past childbearing age, was enabled to bear children because she considered him faithful who had made the promise. And so from this one man, and he as good as dead, came descendants as numerous as the stars in the sky and as countless as the sand on the seashore.*

Who was Sarah?

_____

_____

Consider the timescale for the birth of Isaac:

How old was Abraham when God called him?
Genesis 12:4 _____

How old was Abraham when Sarah gave Hagar to him?
Genesis 16:3 _____

How old was Abraham when Hagar gave birth to Ishmael?
Genesis 16:16

How old was Abraham when God revisited him and changed his name?

Genesis 17:1-2

How old was Abraham when Isaac was born?

Genesis 21:5

How long, in total, did Sarah and Abraham wait for their promise?

Why might Sarah have found this delay more difficult to deal with than Abraham?

Read Genesis 16:1-4.

Why was Sarah's idea to give Hagar to Abraham wrong when it was acceptable according to the custom of that time?

What was the result of Abraham and Sarah's decision to take things into their own hands and what can we learn from this?

Have you ever tried taking matters into your own hands when waiting on God's timing? What happened?

Is there something you have given up hope of happening?

Look up the following verses. What do they tell you about God's timing?

Psalm 27:14	
Romans 5:6	
Ecclesiastes 3:11	
Genesis 18:14	

Read Genesis 18:10-15.

What was Sarah's response when she heard about the promise of a child in one year? What does her response indicate about her faith?

Why do you think Sarah was included in the list of the heroes of faith in Hebrews 11?

How have you seen God do the impossible in your life?

What is your response when God asks you to do something that seems impossible?

Read Genesis 21:1-7.

What does the name Isaac mean?

How do you imagine Sarah's laughter here to be different to her earlier laughter?

Sarah is a wonderful example of someone who doubted God's promise, and yet mastered her doubts to be known as an incredible woman of faith. No matter where we have come from and what we have done, no matter how often we have doubted or failed to believe that God can do what he has said he can do, it's not too late. We can rejoice in the time of waiting, knowing God is faithful, and we can trust in his word.

ABRAHAM

THE TESTING OF FAITH

Let's face it, some Bible verses make better fridge magnets than others. A beautiful picture background, with Jeremiah 29:11 written over it in flowing script, makes for a beautifully encouraging gift:

> *For I know the plans I have for you," declares the LORD, "plans to prosper you and not to harm you, plans to give you hope and a future.*

The recipient may be less impressed if you offer something along the lines of James 1:2-3:

> *Consider it pure joy, my brothers and sisters, whenever you face trials of many kinds, because you know that the testing of your faith produces perseverance.*

I'm not sure that I'd like more trials in my life, thank you very much, regardless of whether they're something to be joyful about! I'm not sure that I like the sound of my faith being tested.

And yet, the Bible repeatedly tells us that our faith will, indeed, be tested. Peter speaks of distressing trials to be faced, our faith being tested as by fire.[4] Isaiah speaks of being tested in the furnace of affliction.[5] Paul is a living example of a trial-filled life, beaten, stoned, shipwrecked, facing dangers wherever he went;[6] it would have been easy for him to give up, and yet he recognised something. The testing of faith may be uncomfortable, it may be painful, it may feel like passing through a furnace of affliction, but it is through those moments that we do, as James explained, develop perseverance. It is in those moments where we have a choice: to walk away from our faith, to extinguish it, or to push through, to set one foot in front of the other, to keep on keeping on, until our faith is activated again. It is often within those trials, those tests, that we see God coming through for us in mighty ways, if we can cling on to him through the storm.

One Bible character springs instantly to mind as we consider the testing of faith, and so we return, again, to the life of Abraham.

On one ordinary, sunny day, Abraham was going about his normal life. Perhaps he was checking over his livestock, meeting with the servants tending his flocks to discuss how things were going. Perhaps he was sitting down to a meal with his beloved wife, Sarah, and his son, Isaac. All of a sudden, God appears, and calls out, 'Abraham!' I'm here, Abraham replies, and God gives this man of faith a new instruction.

> *Then God said, "Take your son, your only son, whom you love—Isaac—and go to the region of Moriah. Sacrifice him there as a burnt offering on a mountain I will show you."*
>
> **-Genesis 22:2-**

Wait just a moment here, God. You want me to take the son I waited twenty-five years for, the fulfilment of a promise that you yourself gave me, and sacrifice him?

It's easy to read the Bible with the benefit of hindsight. We know this story works out okay in the end, but right now I want you to put yourself in Abraham's shoes. He doesn't know the end of this story. Abraham was a real man, with the same emotions and fears and frustrations in life that we feel today. He was not some sort of superhuman being who never felt doubt. I can't even begin to imagine the torment in his heart on hearing this instruction. God wasn't asking him to leave his child and go to a new land again. He wasn't explaining that something tragic and terrible was going to happen to Isaac which would result in his death.

No. God was telling Abraham to take this child, this teenager now, someone big and strong enough to carry the wood on which his own body would be burnt, and sacrifice him with his own hands.

Take a moment to let that sink in.

This is an utterly crazy request that God is making. It is an extraordinary test, and I'm sure Abraham had moments of doubt on his three-day journey to the mountain.

What if I heard wrong?

What if I didn't hear God speaking at all?

What if it was just my imagination?

Perhaps you've asked yourself similar questions in the past, particularly in a time of testing, when the way before you doesn't seem to make any sense, when it feels as though God's direction is pulling you away from a promise he himself has spoken over your life.

Despite any questions or doubts Abraham may have had in light of God's instruction, Hebrews 11 details his response.

> *By faith Abraham, when God tested him, offered Isaac as a sacrifice. He who had embraced the promises was about to sacrifice his one and only son, even though God had said to him, "It is through Isaac that your offspring will be reckoned." Abraham reasoned that God could even raise the dead, and so in a manner of speaking he did receive Isaac back from death."*
>
> **-Hebrews 11:17-19-**

There is so much that we can glean from this story to aid us in our walk of faith today.

Firstly, Abraham knew the character of God. He knew that God is good, that he is faithful to his promises. He had first-hand evidence of that, in having seen God move in a miraculous way to bring laughter into the lives of himself and his wife, a child, born in a way that was not possible. Though Abraham lived before the days of the law, when we begin to realise how utterly despicable God found the practice of child sacrifice which was common at that time, I'm sure Abraham knew it was not in his nature to demand such a thing.

No matter what happens in our lives, we can cling to the goodness of God.

Abraham had seen God's goodness and power in action, and he reasoned, quite logically, that if this was something God was asking him to do, then God would simply have to raise Isaac from the dead after it. I love that in the account of the story itself in Genesis 22, we read:

> *On the third day Abraham looked up and saw the place in the distance. He said to his servants, "Stay here with the donkey while I and the boy go over there. We will worship and then we will come back to you."*
>
> **-Genesis 22:4-5-**

There was no doubt in Abraham's mind that both he and Isaac would return, regardless of what God had asked him to do.

What an amazing revelation he had of who God is.

How much easier would we find it to walk through those trials, those tests, in our lives, if we had the same kind of revelation ourselves? If we were utterly assured of God's goodness and power? There will always be moments when we don't understand the direction in which the journey takes us, but when we can lean fully on God's glorious goodness, those bumps in the road become less all consuming, in light of who he is.

On first reading of Abraham and Isaac's story, that goodness may be in question, when it feels as though God is rubbing salt in the wound. His repetition in his instruction to Abraham seems strange – don't simply take anything to sacrifice, Abraham, take your son, your only son, the one you really, really love, Isaac, the child of the promise, that's the one you're to sacrifice as a burnt offering.

In reality though, God's repetition was more reassurance. Repetition in the Bible typically occurs because those particular words bear special significance. God was reminding Abraham that, yes, he was to take his son, but also to remember the offering was indeed the promised offspring through whom

Abraham's descendants would be reckoned, those offspring who would outnumber the grains of sand in the desert. That couldn't come to pass if Isaac was dead.

God is ever faithful to his word. He doesn't lie. He doesn't change his mind. He will not break his promises.

God wasn't mocking Abraham, laughing at what he'd have to give up. He was reminding him of his own faithfulness. To paraphrase: 'I gave you this child whom you love, Abraham. Trust me. You're still going to see the fulfilment of every promise I have made to you.'

What a reassurance to us, today. We can count on God's promises. We can count on God's word. The Bible isn't simply a nice book for us to read: it is a guarantee God is for us, that he is with us, that he is actively involved in our lives, that he cares about the details of what happens in our each and every day.

> *For no matter how many promises God has made, they are "Yes" in Christ. And so through him the "Amen" is spoken by us to the glory of God.*
>
> **-2 Corinthians 1:20-**

An English translation of the word 'amen' is 'so be it'. When we finish a prayer with 'amen', we are agreeing to what we've just said. We can say the same to the promises of God. When he promises, we can say, with full confidence in his goodness, his power, his ability to bring about what he has promised, 'so be it'.

Even with that knowledge, this was still not going to be an easy journey for Abraham, but God had one final reassurance for him.

> "... Sacrifice him there as a burnt offering on a mountain I will show you."
>
> **-Genesis 22:2b-**

If this sounds somewhat familiar, it's because we looked at a verse phrased in a very similar way only two chapters ago.

> The LORD had said to Abram, "Go from your country, your people and your father's household to the land I will show you."
>
> **-Genesis 12:1-**

In his brief instruction to Abraham to take Isaac to the mountain, God was reminding Abraham of another time when he had stepped out in faith, and God had come through for him. Once again, Abraham was stepping into the unknown, walking to an unknown destination, with unknown consequences. Isn't that beautiful? God knows us, he understands us, he recognises when we need a little extra reassurance.

But this also demonstrates that God grows us a bit at a time. This request to sacrifice his own son didn't come at the very outset of Abraham's relationship with God – it came after Abraham had seen God fulfil his promises over and over. This particular test was one of the last that Abraham would have in his life, or one of the last we know of, at least. As we get better at activating our faith, at trusting through the wind and the waves, those waves will get bigger, and our faith will be stretched again, until it's ready to face an even greater storm.

That might sound challenging, but it's thrilling. God loves us so dearly, and holds us so gently, that he will test us only in such a way that he knows we can come through to the other side.

I vividly remember hearing a preacher speak once, explaining that faith is like a balloon. It can be a challenge to blow it up that first time, but if you allow the air out and blow the balloon up again, it will be easier. Once our faith has been stretched, it will stretch more easily the next time. I love that picture. We don't need more faith today, but the elasticity of our faith will grow with each test, with each trial, until we are able to trust God in anything and everything.

Perhaps you've heard those stories of super-Christians trusting God through sickness or struggle without even a waver in their faith, of missionaries stepping into completely unknown encounters to share the love of Christ, of martyrs who have stood boldly, refusing to renounce their belief in Almighty God to save their own lives. It can be easy to think that they are a different breed of Christian, that their faith is much greater than your own. That's not the case. In each instance, if you look back over their lives, you will see the moments where their faith was tested, where they stood, holding to the goodness of God, until they saw the one who is faithful, who fulfils all of his promises. The next time, they were able to stand more easily, and so on.

Your faith is not inferior to anyone else's, but it is only through times of testing where you will see it stretch. God is not asking you to take your child up a hill with a knife and a lighter today, but you will face tests in each day of your life. Will you live according to the word or the world? Will you stand against unrighteousness, even if it costs you? Will you continue to hold to truth when you receive news that seems impossible to bear? It's in those moments, through our darkest days, when our relationships with God can grow deeper. This is how it is possible to rejoice when trials come. If God is truly the most important thing in our lives, then we can rejoice in any situation which will strengthen our union with him, which will stretch our faith, even if it is painful at the time.

That's not to say that we should never mourn, or pray for resolution to our problems because we're growing through them. It's not to say we shouldn't expect to see the miraculous at work in our lives because we're going through a time of testing. God miraculously provided a ram, after all. It is to say that whatever we face in our lives, good or bad, in a time of testing or a time of plenty, we can put our trust in God our Saviour, and remain confident he holds our lives in the palm of his hand.

I don't know what the tests will look like for you, but I know that God does not break his promises. He will bring you to where you need to be in the end. All we see is the little part of our lives we're living in right now, but God, he sees the whole picture, the end and the beginning, and he will bring you into the promise he has spoken over your life. God cares about the promises he has spoken to you, as much as he cared about the promise he made to Abraham. Hold fast, if it seems your dream lies in tatters on the floor. Hold fast, if it seems God's guidance is taking you in a direction that's the opposite of what you hoped to achieve in your life. He has it in hand, and you can, and will, receive your own dream, your promise, back from death.

Questions for Further Study

Background reading:

Hebrews 11:17-19

Genesis 22:1-19

What did God ask Abraham to do?

How did Abraham respond? Would you have responded the same way?

How many days did the journey take? Why wouldn't God tell Abraham to offer Isaac as a sacrifice where they were?

What does this tell you about Abraham's faith?

What are some of the reasons God tested Abraham at this point in his life, after he had already waited patiently to see the promise of God?

How can we know for sure if an instruction is from God?

Is it okay for us to question God in how/why he is doing something? Explain your answer.

Read Genesis 22:5 and Hebrews 11:19.
What do these verses tell us about Abraham's view of God?

What do the following verses tell us about the testing of our faith?

James 1:2-3	
James 1:12-13	
Isaiah 48:10	
1 Peter 1:6-7	
Job 7:17-18	
1 Peter 4:12	

Did any of these verses particularly stand out to you? Why?

How does God practically test our faith today?

Is every difficult circumstance in our lives a test from God?

What is your response to God in a time of testing?

Are there any areas where God has been testing you? How is your character developing in those areas?

Read Mark 10:17-22.
How was this young man tested?

Just like Abraham, the young man was asked to give up something dear to him. We don't know what Jesus would have said if his answer had been different – perhaps the request to give up his wealth was the test, but he wasn't willing to relinquish it.

What are other things we might struggle to surrender fully to God?

_____

_____

_____

Is there anything specific you would struggle to sacrifice if God asked you to?

_____

_____

_____

God tested Abraham, asking him to make an incredible sacrifice. It can be hard for us to understand how God could ever ask something so seemingly barbaric of a faithful follower, but Abraham knew the character of God and he knew the promises of God. Sometimes it can feel like we're really being refined in the fire, but if we can hold faithfully to the truth of who God is and what he has promised to do in our lives, we will always come through stronger than we were.

ISAAC

GENERATIONAL FAITH

'And what do you do?'

It's the first question I'm asked whenever we talk about our life as missionaries. Dave is an aircraft engineer; among his many and varied roles within Mission Aviation Fellowship is the fundamental core of fixing planes, so that they can fly weird and wonderful cargo (and people) to the remotest corners of the world. It's something tangible which people can understand. It's a vital role in an organisation which is helping to spread the gospel message and practical aid.

'But what about you, Becky? What do you do?'

I used to struggle with that question a lot. It's all too easy for our worth, our identity, to be tied into the things we do, the tasks we achieve, the items we tick off our to-do lists. We like to be recognised for our achievements. It's easy to feel that fighting with laundry when there's no water or electricity supply, and trying to cook dinner when the food you wanted to buy is nowhere to be found, isn't quite as important as the crucial work of fixing an engine for a life-saving flight.

This isn't some new fad, something that's only crept into our society in the last few years; there has always been a desire for our work to be seen as important, for our greatness to be acknowledged. Even Jesus' own hand-picked disciples fell into this trap.

> *An argument started among the disciples as to which of them would be the greatest.*
>
> **-Luke 9:46-**

Jesus lets them know that it is in fact the least who will become the greatest in this upside-down kingdom he is bringing to the world. And yet, it seems these closest of followers didn't exactly learn their lesson. In their final moments with Jesus, sharing the Last Supper together, they return to the same old argument.

> *A dispute also arose among them as to which of them was considered to be greatest.*
>
> **-Luke 22:24-**

It seems to be part of the human condition to want to receive accolades for our best work, to be known among the great. Humility is perhaps one of the more difficult character traits we are to develop as followers of Jesus.

A part of this desire to be noticed, to be considered great, is comparison. Our greatness can only be measured against the people around us. The dawn of social media has made comparison an even greater threat. We are bombarded with images showcasing snippets of other people's lives. I've chuckled with the rest of us at parody videos showing Christians preparing the perfect photo for Instagram – line the Bible up just so, make sure it's open to a good verse, turn on the perfect mood lighting, arrange the cup of coffee at the right angle to the Bible and snap. We don't see the preparation, only the final photo of this holier-than-thou Christian, so very devoted to the Scriptures. As we compare ourselves with that brief moment in time, we perhaps feel that we aren't so successful in our walk with God. Or our thoughts may shift in the other direction, and we feel better than that person, not having to show off about our quiet time with Jesus, and a little pride creeps into our hearts.

Comparison is dangerous.

Comparison can deactivate our faith.

It doesn't matter what the world says about us. It doesn't matter how our greatness (or lack thereof) compares with the people around us. All that matters is who God says we are: beloved children, fearfully and wonderfully made, created for a unique purpose.

When I glance through the list of the Heroes of Faith we are considering through the course of this book, I find it very easy to dismiss a man called Isaac. He always feels like a bridge character in the story of the patriarchs, stuffed in between Abraham, the father of faith, and Jacob, who would become Israel, the head of the twelve tribes.

Isaac is perhaps not the first character who would spring to mind as you think of those in the Bible who lived by faith, yet there were many moments in his life where he showed complete and absolute trust in God.

This was a man who, as a strapping youth, walked up a hill with his aged father, carrying the very wood that was to be used to burn his own body. He wasn't a toddler in this tale. Abraham, his father, was well over 100 at this point; I'm pretty confident that Isaac could have overpowered him. This gives a new perspective on the story, showing us a young man who willingly lay down on a rock and allowed his father to bind him. A man who would have willingly sacrificed himself at God's request. That mountain moment was a significant test of faith for Abraham, yes, but also for Isaac.

As we read on in his story, we hear of the miraculous moment when a servant sets out for the distant land where the remainder of Abraham's family lives, to seek out a wife for Isaac. I'm sure his parents had a say in the matter, but Isaac still chose not to settle for the women who lived around him, women who may have turned his heart from the God of his father. Instead, he waited for the right person who God wanted him to be with. Remember, Isaac was forty years old when he married Rebekah; he could certainly have taken the opportunity in those years to find a different wife.

We hear of a familiar sadness in the tale. Rebekah is unable to have children, unable to bring grandchildren to Abraham from whom there should be descendants as numerous as the stars in the sky. Does Isaac take another wife when he discovers this fact? No. Does he follow his father's example, and beget a child with a slave woman? No.

> *Isaac prayed to the LORD on behalf of his wife, because she was childless. The LORD answered his prayer, and his wife Rebekah became pregnant.*
>
> **-Genesis 25:21-**

There are some incredible moments of activated faith in this story. Isaac faced a time of famine too, as his father did. Instead of running off to Egypt like Abraham, Isaac stayed in the place God had told him to be, despite the difficulties it might cause, and we see his faith dramatically rewarded.

> *Isaac planted crops in that land and the same year reaped a hundredfold, because the LORD blessed him.*
>
> **-Genesis 26:12-**

In a year of famine, when crops were failing and people were starving, Isaac obeyed God, planted his seed, and reaped a hundredfold what he planted. He saw a mind-blowing miracle, because he acted in faith.

Isaac wasn't perfect. The Bible documents his mistakes as well, but there are shining moments on the road he walked where he truly acted from a position of faith. Isaac never had a permanent home; he lived in tents, like his father before him, and he kept hope in that future promise, that one day the land would belong to him and his offspring.

However, despite those achievements, despite those wonderful miracles and a life punctuated by moments of incredible faith, this is what Isaac is remembered for in the faith annals:

> *By faith Isaac blessed Jacob and Esau in regard to their future.*
>
> **-Hebrews 11:20-**

It's the shortest entry of all in the series, and it's one that seems to ignore all of those amazing deeds, those things he could argue his case for in a competition of who was the greatest among the patriarchs. If I was Isaac, I think I'd be tapping on the shoulder of the author of Hebrews and demanding an explanation.

In actuality though, this little line has much to teach us about faith and humility.

For the first time in Hebrews 11, we read about a character who is remembered for something that doesn't directly concern himself and the life he was living. Abel worshipped God, Enoch walked with him, Noah built an ark to save himself and his family, Abraham followed God and he and Sarah believed for their miracle baby. All of those faith-filled activities relate to their own personal walks with God, with the actions they took during their own lives.

All of those faith-filled activities are crucial to our own lives. We need to worship God, to walk with him, to take action, to trust as we step into the unknown and through the wait and in the test. I don't think it's a coincidence that we learn those lessons first through our study of Hebrews 11. Our journey to activated faith begins with implementing those personal strategies within our own lives. And then, when we reach the point of trusting God with what's happening in front of our noses, we can begin to have the faith to look beyond ourselves, the faith to look forward.

There are only a couple of recorded moments when God spoke directly to Isaac, but in one of them he reiterated the wonderful promise he had made to Abraham.

> *I will make your descendants as numerous as the stars in the sky and will give them all these lands, and through your offspring all nations on earth will be blessed.*
>
> **-Genesis 26:4-**

By the end of his life, however, Isaac only had two children: Esau and Jacob. Those two certainly weren't as numerous as the stars in the sky, and yet, when Isaac was close to death, he took the chance to bless his offspring, believing absolutely that the promise would be fulfilled. That is why he is remembered as a man of faith. He believed God would do exactly what he had said, and if he wasn't going to see the fulfilment of the promise with his own eyes? That was okay, because he could still pray that blessing over his children for their future. He had faith that the next generation would take the baton and run the race God had called them to.

It was for building up and blessing the next generation that Isaac was added to this list of faith-filled characters.

At some point, we need to realise that activated faith reaches much further than our own lives. It is something which can impact future generations, something which can spark revivals, something which can believe and hope for the salvation of a nation. Isaac could only see his two sons, but he believed for multitudes.

I wonder how often we find ourselves praying for something similar? Do we believe that God can powerfully impact the generations coming behind us? Or do we simply bemoan their strange ways of doing things, be they Millennials or Gen Z or Gen Alpha or whatever comes next? It may not be something we see in our lifetimes, but that shouldn't stop us investing into it with prayer. With his own eyes, Isaac couldn't see millions of descendants with the potential to bless every nation on earth, but through the eyes of faith, he could believe it.

It is important for us to think about the future. Not to the point where we stop living in the present, or spend all our time worrying about what is to come, but we should be thinking of and praying for the futures of those people around us. We should be investing into, blessing and encouraging our children, our mentees, the youth in our churches. No matter how old or young you are, you can always lift someone up who is coming behind you.

What can you do in your life right now to spur other people on to love and good deeds? How can you help another person to finish the race well? What can you leave that will live on in the life of others? Leaving a legacy is not about having your name on a plaque for a donation you might have made, it's about your life inspiring others to live their lives with activated faith, ready and expectant to see God move in miraculous ways.

Words are powerful things. If you read through the book of Genesis, you'll know Isaac's blessing didn't exactly go the way he'd wanted it to. Isaac was deceived by his wife Rebekah and son Jacob, to ensure that the better blessing went to the secondborn, leaving Esau out in the cold. The secondary blessing Esau was left with was so disappointing to him that it festered into anger, and he determined to murder his own brother, who was forced to flee for his life. Esau eventually forgave Jacob, but he bore a grudge against his brother for many years.

We don't know if the words of Isaac's blessings were specifically given by God or something he had prepared. The Bible isn't entirely clear on that. But it is clear that the words spoken over Esau negatively affected his life and relationships. There is a lot of power in the words we speak.

> *The tongue also is a fire, a world of evil among the parts of the body. It corrupts the whole body, sets the whole course of one's life on fire, and is itself set on fire by hell.*
>
> **-James 3:6-**

James speaks of this uncontrollable, restless evil, full of deadly poison – the tongue. Something so small can do so much damage. Words can't be taken back once spoken. That's a good reason for us to consider carefully what we are saying. Are your words building someone up, or tearing someone down? Are you inspiring the next generation to greater works, or telling them their dream, their call, can never be fulfilled?

> *... through your offspring all nations on earth will be blessed.*
>
> **-Genesis 26:4-**

Isaac's offspring were blessed to be a blessing. As God's chosen people today, a royal priesthood, a holy nation, God's special possession, we are also called to be a blessing to this dark world. We don't need to wait until we're on our deathbeds to speak blessing. We can do it right now. We can invest ourselves for the sake of others, be it through our words, through our finance, through our work, or through any other means. You are called to have an impact on this world. You are called to put down self, and to lift up others.

When we think of faith, it's easy to think we need to do something amazing. We need to be like Noah and build our ark. We need to be like Abraham and willing to surrender everything. And yet, Isaac shows us there is as much value, if not more, in having the faith to push the next generation on to bigger and better things, even if, in the process, we ourselves are overlooked.

This world will tell us that we need to be remembered. It will tell us that we need to ensure everyone knows we are the greatest. It will tell us that this life we live is all about us. And yet, Isaac's example brings to mind those beautiful and powerful words of John the Baptist.

> *He must become greater; I must become less."*
> -John 3:30-

For what would you most like to be remembered? Something that benefitted you in your lifetime? Or something that inspired greatness in others, to ultimately bring glory to our great God?

Activate your faith today, and believe God will work wonders and do what he has promised, even if you don't get to see the results.

Questions for Further Study

Background reading:

Hebrews 11:20
Genesis 27

What do we know about Isaac? What sort of a life did he live?

_____

_____

_____

Why was blessing his two sons an act of faith?

_____

_____

_____

Summarise what happened when Isaac blessed his children. (Genesis 27)

_____

_____

What does it make you think about these characters?

Isaac: _____

Rebekah: _____

Jacob: _____

Esau: _____

Did their actions and responses show faith in God? In what way?

_____

_____

_____

Isaac was distressed when he realised he had blessed Jacob instead of Esau, and yet he continued to trust in God and accepted what had happened.

Do you ever find yourself feeling bitter if things don't work out as you'd expected them to?

_____

_____

How can we trust God when it seems his instructions contradict what we think is the right way to do something?

Read Genesis 25:21-23 and Genesis 27:29.

What did God tell Rebekah about the futures of her children?

It's probably safe to assume Rebekah would have told her husband, Isaac, about this word from God, and yet how does Isaac go on to bless the man he thinks is Esau?

Why might he have done that?

Is it harder to obey God's instructions when they seem at odds with the views of our culture or society? Why?

How can we get better at listening to God's instruction over any other influences?

Things might not have worked out quite the way Isaac intended, and yet he is still recorded as a man of faith for blessing Jacob and Esau in regard to their future.

What was the significance about speaking a blessing concerning their future?

How can we speak into the future of the generations coming after us?

What do these verses say is our responsibility to those around us and future generations?

Psalm 145:4	
Deuteronomy 6:6-7	
Psalm 78:4	
Psalm 102:18	
2 Timothy 1:3-5	
Psalm 71:18	

What can you apply from these verses to your own life in a practical way?

Isaac was known as a man of faith because he looked further than the end of his own days. In faith, he spoke into the lives of his children, that they would be blessed and would have their own faith in God. It's a challenge to us to do the same. Whether or not God is calling us to some great act of faith in our lives, we all have the opportunity to encourage and inspire the generations coming after us to do even greater things for God's kingdom.

JACOB

FAITH TO FINISH WELL

As an avid reader, I've always found the very best characters in books are flawed. We don't like to read about people who are perfect. We like to read about people who overcame their obstacles, who grew into their potential, who turned from darkness to light. Other than Jesus – God himself come down to earth – there has never been a perfect person. We are all of us flawed (sorry to be the one to let you know, if you weren't aware).

The great news is that God takes us, imperfect humanity, and works through us. You don't need to be perfect to do great things. You don't need to be perfect to have faith.

Hebrews 11 contains a wonderful array of imperfect people commended for achieving great things by faith. It's true, there are the Enochs and the Noahs, upstanding men in their own communities, but there are also the Abrahams and the Isaacs, both of whom put their wives in awkward and potentially dangerous positions to save their own skins. We have Sarah, who outright laughed in the face of God at the thought of the promise he had given her. God looks at these people, this array of flawed humanity, and says these are my people, these are people of faith.

God looks beyond our mistakes, beyond our doubts, beyond our catastrophic mess-ups. He sees those moments when we did obey, even when we didn't know what was going to happen, when we did act, simply because he told us to, when we did trust, even when the promise seemed impossible. It's in those moments, not the former, where I can picture God grabbing an angel by the arm, pointing to earth and saying, 'Look! Have you seen my son? My daughter? Look how faithful they are!' What a wonder that is. He truly is a God of mercy and grace, and his forgiveness is enough to cover our greatest faults.

When you think about flawed characters in the Bible, our next foray into Hebrews 11 is certainly someone who fits the bill. Jacob lied, he deceived his own brother and father, he was a man who, it seemed, would do anything for his own gain, no matter what it may cost those around him. His very name, Jacob, meant supplanter, deceiver. He was selfish, cunning, a trickster.

This is a man God chose to use. This is a man in the lineage of Jesus. This is a man commended for his great faith.

> *By faith Jacob, when he was dying, blessed each of Joseph's sons, and worshiped as he leaned on the top of his staff.*
>
> **-Hebrews 11:21-**

What story arc took Jacob from a man busy looking out for only himself, into a man who would worship with his last breath? What changed in this man, that at the end of his life he would bless not only his own sons, but also his grandsons, speaking into their future and commending them to keep up the worship of the God of their ancestors?

The answer is found, in part, as Jacob flees for his life, running from the land of his birth to a place called Harran, where the remainder of Abraham's family still dwelt. Jacob had stolen his brother Esau's blessing in an elaborate ruse, dressing himself up in Esau's clothes and even putting goat skin on his arms and neck to appear hairier. To say Esau was unimpressed would be an understatement; his anger burnt so hotly he decided to kill his brother Jacob.

As he runs, Jacob stops for the night, uses a stone for a pillow and drifts into sleep.

> *He had a dream in which he saw a stairway resting on the earth, with its top reaching to heaven, and the angels of God were ascending and descending on it. There above it stood the LORD, and he said: "I am the LORD, the God of your father Abraham and the God of Isaac. I will give you and your descendants the land on which you are lying. Your descendants will be like the dust of the earth, and you will spread out to the west and to the east, to the north and to the south. All peoples on earth will be blessed through you and your offspring. I am with you and will watch over you wherever you go, and I will bring you back to this land. I will not leave you until I have done what I have promised you."*
>
> **-Genesis 28:12-15-**

This, to a man on the run for his life because of his trickster ways. Jacob's response is beautiful.

> *When Jacob awoke from his sleep, he thought, "Surely the LORD is in this place, and I was not aware of it." He was afraid and said, "How awesome is this place! This is none other than the house of God; this is the gate of heaven."*
>
> **-Genesis 28:16-17-**

An encounter with the living God can't help but change us. Jacob saw heaven literally touching earth, and in that moment, he was transformed. The power of an encounter with God will not leave us the same as we were before it. In that very moment, Jacob sets up his stone pillow as a pillar, and makes a promise to God.

> *Then Jacob made a vow, saying, "If God will be with me and will watch over me on this journey I am taking and will give me food to eat and clothes to wear so that I return safely to my father's household, then the LORD will be my God and this stone that I have set up as a pillar will be God's house, and of all that you give me I will give you a tenth."*
>
> **-Genesis 28:20-22-**

This is a dramatic turnaround. Jacob, the man out for himself, freely offers God a tenth of all he will ever have, even though God doesn't make that request of him. In this moment, Jacob expresses his heart to make the Lord his own God, not simply the God of his father and grandfather.

Jacob wasn't perfect from this moment on, but he was changed. His vow was still coloured with a hint of selfishness (if you bless me, then I'll give back to you), but there was an undeniable attitude shift at this point in his life. Jacob was not a reputable man, but God saw the potential in him, and woke him up with an encounter with the King of Kings.

God linked heaven and earth for us too, when he sent his son to die for us on a cross. We must not fail to let that encounter change us. God sees the potential in you too; there is nothing so bad that you may have done in your life that the sacrifice of Jesus can't cover. Some of Jacob's actions were despicable, and yet through his encounter with God, he recognised that he was not beyond redemption. Your own encounter with God can change the course of your life, if you will let it.

As you read on into the life of Jacob, you'll find numerous instances where he worships God, has encounters with God, even wrestles with God. Jacob's own name is changed; no longer is he the deceiver – now he's known as Israel, the namesake of a nation. When Jacob returns to the land of Canaan years later, he spurs his own family on to worship God, to rid themselves of any idols and to follow the one true Lord.

Jacob's life was marked by worship after he had an encounter with God. That's what he's commended for: having faith to worship to the end. His faith was no less strong at the point of death than it was in life. Even in that moment where he was all but blind, confined to his bed, his earthly usefulness seemingly at an end, he worshipped. What an example that set for his children, his grandchildren. My body may be weak, this life may be over, but with all the strength remaining to me, I choose to worship.

As long as you have a breath in your body with which to praise our great God, your usefulness is far from over.

There are many things in this world which will threaten to steal your faith. The enemy wants nothing more than for you to surrender your trust in God, to fail to live a life of worship, to fill you with fear at the prospect of death, feeling that you haven't achieved enough or lived a good enough life for God. He wants you to leave this earth despondent, not praising and certainly not passing a blessing on to anyone else.

Not only did Jacob have the faith to worship as he lay dying, but also to bless each of Joseph's sons. Even at the end of his days, he looked forward to what God would do through this future generation, just as his father Isaac had done, as we considered in the previous chapter.

Curiously though, Hebrews 11 doesn't commend Jacob for blessing his own sons, though he did that too, but rather the sons of Joseph, two of his grandchildren. Why did this require greater faith than speaking into the lives of his own children?

In that moment, Jacob chose to reckon Joseph's first two children, Ephraim and Manasseh, as his own. In other words, they would receive a blessing equal to the actual sons of Jacob. By granting this blessing, creating two new tribes within the nation of Israel, Jacob was effectively giving Joseph the rights of the firstborn son, allocating him a double portion of the inheritance. This was common practice at the time; the firstborn would receive double compared with all the other siblings. That was part of the reason Esau had been so angry at Jacob for duping him out of the blessing of the firstborn – it was worth twice as much.

The actual firstborn son of Jacob, Reuben, was not in Jacob's good books after committing a detestable act and sleeping with one of his father's concubines while his father was still alive.[7] He was still the firstborn, however, and choosing to pass him by, to offer the double portion to another son, was counter to the culture at the time.

There may be times when our own steps of faith clash with our cultures. In these days where it seems near impossible to speak without offending somebody, we may need to risk giving offence to stick to the truth of the word. Much of what Jesus preached is counter-cultural. It's all too easy to live with one foot in the world and one foot in the word, but that's not the life of faith we're called to live.

As if granting the rights of the firstborn to a younger son wasn't enough, Jacob went on to bless the younger grandson ahead of the older – another convention-defying moment. It was one that had the potential to drive a rift between Jacob and the son who had been lost to him for so many years – his favourite, Joseph. Jacob was willing to risk it, to deliver the blessing God had ordained him to bring.

At times when we need to act in faith, the hardest opposition we can face may come from those closest to us. It is always important to listen to the advice and concerns of our nearest and dearest, but we must weigh those opinions against what God has told us to do. It's easy to be swayed by the people who love us, but there will be moments when we need to stick to our guns, and continue to step forward in faith. Around the world today, there are many Christians who have faced shunning, disowning, even persecution from their own families for daring to follow Jesus. There is sometimes a great cost to following God.

> *Then he [Jesus] said to them all: "Whoever wants to be my disciple must deny themselves and take up their cross daily and follow me. For whoever wants to save their life will lose it, but whoever loses their life for me will save it. What good is it for someone to gain the whole world, and yet lose or forfeit their very self?"*
>
> **-Luke 9:23-25-**

There are so many wonderful verses in Scripture that speak of God's blessing to us, that it can be easy to forget this is not always an easy road. Jesus himself promises that in this life we will have trouble,[8] and yet, in the midst of it, we are also promised peace and assurance that, though we may need to suffer a little while, he has overcome the world and the troubles we face within it. Victory belongs to Jesus, and the battle is already won. That is a faith-strengthening reminder, and one we can cling to in those moments where we need to take up our cross, in those moments where our faith prompts us to stand for something that our culture, and even our family and friends, would criticise.

It takes faith to finish well.

It takes faith to hang on to the promises of God throughout your life.

Jacob didn't have an easy run to his finish line. He had to endure believing one of his sons was dead. He lived through a severe famine. He had to pack up his entire life and move to the nation of Egypt, a place he had never visited. It was not plain sailing, even after an encounter with God, even after making the choice to worship through the hardship.

> *Therefore, since we are surrounded by such a great cloud of witnesses, let us throw off everything that hinders and the sin that so easily entangles. And let us run with perseverance the race marked out for us, fixing our eyes on Jesus, the pioneer and perfecter of faith.*
>
> **-Hebrews 12:1-2a-**

Running a race is not easy. It's tiring. It's hard work. There will be moments where we simply want to stop. And yet, we can keep running, keep worshipping, continue to invest in and encourage others, when we keep our eyes fixed on Jesus, the one who is working in us to perfect our faith.

There will be many moments of finishing in your life. Yes, there's the end-of-life moment, as we've considered with Jacob, but there will be times where we finish with a project, with a relationship, with a job, with a geographical location. In every ending, we can finish well, by following Jacob's example: being an encouragement to the people around us, blessing them, trusting that God will hold their future, and continuing to worship as we move into the next phase of our own lives.

In every hardship, every difficult moment, every faith-testing trial, every painful goodbye, those principles will help to keep our faith activated, to turn our eyes once more to Jesus, knowing he is cheering us on.

Questions for Further Study

Background reading:
Hebrews 11:21
Genesis 47:28 – 48:22

What do we know about Jacob and the life that he lived?

What can we learn about the end of Jacob's life from Hebrews 11:21?

Why do you think Jacob is remembered for blessing the children of his son, Joseph?

Read Genesis 41:50-52.

Manassah and Ephraim were born to Joseph in Egypt, to the man who was the second highest in command of the entire nation. Chances are they lived in a palace, surrounded by a culture alien to their extended family, and hearing about gods other than the God of Abraham, Isaac and Jacob, from their mother if no one else.

Does this change the significance of Jacob's action in blessing them? How?

Read Genesis 48:17-19.

What is Joseph's reaction when his father blesses the firstborn son after the secondborn?

Why might this have been hard for Jacob to do?

Can you think of an example when well-meaning friends or relatives have called into question something you felt God telling you to do? How did you handle it?

Read Genesis 47:7-9.

How old was Jacob when he arrived in Egypt?

What was his outlook on life at this point?

Read Genesis 47:28 and 48:15-16.

How old was Jacob when he died?

How had Jacob's outlook on life changed by this point?

Why might this change have occurred?

In Hebrews 11:21 we are told that Jacob was dying, and that, by faith, he worshipped as he leaned on the top of his staff.

What does this tell us about worship?

Why is Jacob commended for worshipping at the end of his life?

Despite what happened throughout the rest of his life, Jacob was faithful at the end. He ran the race well and finished strong.

How can we apply that principle to our own lives?

What can we learn from the following verses about keeping our faith strong to the end?

2 Timothy 4:6-8	
Acts 20:24	
Philippians 3:12-14	
Philippians 1:6	
Galatians 6:9	
Hebrews 12:1	

As Jacob leaned on his staff and worshipped, he undoubtedly looked back over his life to those times when God had come through for him. Remembering how God has impacted our past can help us keep our faith strong in the future. What great things has God done in your life? Write them down and let the memory of them spur you on to worship him.

Jacob was a flawed man, with a character that left a lot to be desired. But despite that, he is recorded among the great men and women of faith because, despite it all, he recognised how amazing his God was, and worshipped with his last breath. Wherever we have come from, wherever we are going, we can learn a lesson from this man of faith – to hold on to the promise God has given us and to never stop praising his wonderful name.

JOSEPH

FAITH FOR THE FUTURE

The future can be an uncertain and terrifying prospect.

In the year 2021, Dave and I were preparing to leave Uganda to move across the continent of Africa to Liberia, stopping for three months in England on the way to catch up with friends and family and supporters of our ministry. With a couple of months left until our leaving date, Dave jumped on a plane to spend three weeks in Liberia assisting with work there, while I concentrated on packing up our lives in Uganda.

Within those three weeks, Uganda announced a severe Covid-19 lockdown; it's very difficult to try to sell a car and other possessions when no one is allowed to leave their homes! Dave, in Liberia, caught Covid himself, far from any home comforts, and resulting in an extra two weeks overseas to mess with our already tight timescale. We also discovered we would need to quarantine in a hotel once we set foot on British soil, as Uganda was considered a red-list country.

The future looked bleak.

These days, I can look back on that time and marvel at how everything fit together so perfectly. Dave did recover, and in the three weeks after his return and before we left Uganda for good, we were able to get everything organised. We sold the car to the first person interested in it, for exactly the asking price. Our goods ended up packed into boxes which arrived in Liberia on the same day we did. It was nothing short of a miracle. Even the mandatory hotel quarantine upon landing in London served us well, as ten days to recover from the craziness of that busy and stressful time.

Everything worked out for the best, but it didn't feel as though it was going to at the time. Hindsight is a wonderful thing, but sadly not something we have access to in the moment where the future looks bleak, and we question how God could ever make a way through the darkness or the sickness or the confusion or the loss.

Having faith for the future is a very real challenge.

When the young Joseph had a dream as a teenager, that his family would one day bow down before him, I can imagine his thoughts for the future. Perhaps I'll become a leader here, in the land of Canaan. Perhaps I will be the first king of this small people group that is my family.

Instead, Joseph finds himself dropped into a dark and damp cistern by his own brothers, perhaps hearing their voices drift down to him as they spoke of murder, as they decided, eventually, to sell him as a slave. The seventeen-year-old Joseph is chained, his freedom stolen by his own flesh and blood, and he is taken to the foreign land of Egypt. Sold into the household of Potiphar, the attractive young man is forced to fend off the advances of his master's wife, and is thrown into prison as his reward.

This entire story takes place across four chapters in the book of Genesis. It's so quick for us to read that it's easy to forget this slavery and imprisonment went on for thirteen long years.

Thirteen years of dealing with the trauma of being sold into slavery by his own brothers. Thirteen years of hardship and loss, away from the familiarity of his father, his own culture and language. Thirteen years of questioning why God would have let this happen to him, how those dreams of his were ever to be fulfilled when they looked so very far away.

I'm sure there were moments in that dark time, in that dreary prison cell, when Joseph felt angry at God, when he doubted the dream for his future, when he felt confused, devastated and lost. We see the positive character traits of Joseph throughout his story, but he was still human, and I can't believe he didn't shed a few tears on his most difficult days.

And yet, despite it all, Joseph did continue to trust God for his future. We know this, because he trusted God in his present. In both Potiphar's house and in an Egyptian prison, Joseph repeatedly rose through the ranks until he was running both of those places. He was still a slave, still imprisoned, but still living under God's favour even in those positions. He continued to stand on the promises of God, even when all his eyes could see were the bars of his prison cell.

Do you trust God with your future? It's easy to say "Yes, of course I do!" We know that's the correct response. But if you really consider that question, it's perhaps not so easy to answer. There are so many things vying for our attention on earth, so many voices shouting about all the things we need to fear. Climate change and economies collapsing and the threat of future global pandemics and the potential for world wars; those are messages we see plastered over the news and our social media profiles. And that's before we start with the personal worries. What will life be like as we grow older? What will happen to our children when we're gone? How will we meet the needs of the next few days and weeks and months and years? Are we really living the lives God has called us to live? Are we in his calling? Are we in the right position to find the future he has in mind for us?

We could spend every moment of our lives fearing for the future. Many people do. Jesus speaks of a better way.

> *Therefore do not worry about tomorrow, for tomorrow will worry about itself. Each day has enough trouble of its own.*
>
> **-Matthew 6:34-**

Don't worry, Jesus says, not about tomorrow, not about any tomorrow to come. Live in this day, in the present. You don't need to be concerned about what you will eat or drink or wear; your heavenly Father knows you need those things, says Jesus,[9] and he will provide.

> *Do not be anxious about anything, but in every situation, by prayer and petition, with thanksgiving, present your requests to God. And the peace of God, which transcends all understanding, will guard your hearts and your minds in Christ Jesus.*
>
> **-Philippians 4:6-7-**

It's a good thing for us to present our requests to God, the Bible instructs us to do just that. You'll notice there's no guarantee of immediately receiving those things we ask for, but there is a guarantee our very hearts and minds will be guarded by peace, the moment we come to God in prayer, with thanksgiving. Wouldn't that be a better way to live? Whenever a fear for the future creeps up, be it the near or distant future, to be able to commit that thing to God in prayer, and then to rest in absolute peace, knowing we don't need to worry about it, knowing that worrying about it won't add a single hour to our lives.

That is the kind of peace Joseph found in the prison.

It's the kind of peace we can live with, in each day of our lives.

If you read on in Joseph's story, you'll discover that everything works out in the end. He is freed from prison and made second in command of the very powerful nation of Egypt, making him one of the most important men in the entire world. He doesn't need to worry about what he'll eat or drink or wear any more. And yet, even in that place of comfort and plenty, we see Joseph is still trusting God with the future.

> *By faith Joseph, when his end was near, spoke about the exodus of the Israelites from Egypt and gave instructions concerning the burial of his bones.*
>
> **-Hebrews 11:22-**

At the end of his life, Joseph placed the future of his people into the hands of God. Just as he could trust the dream he was given as a teenager would one day come to pass, so he could trust in the word God had spoken about his people. I wonder how many times, in his prison cell, Joseph reminded himself of that beautiful promise spoken by God to Abraham and Isaac and Jacob, that they would be a people through whom God would impact the world. It must have been something to cling on to, even in the midst of uncertainty, anguish and fear. We can see Joseph's amazing trust in God echoing through the words he spoke at this moment, concluding the book of Genesis.

> *Then Joseph said to his brothers, "I am about to die. But God will surely come to your aid and take you up out of this land to the land he promised on oath to Abraham, Isaac and Jacob." And Joseph made the Israelites swear an oath and said, "God will surely come to your aid, and then you must carry my bones up from this place.".*
>
> **-Genesis 50:24-25-**

Joseph was so very convinced that God would bring his people out of Egypt in the future that he did more than simply encourage them to keep believing: he made them promise to take his bones to bury them in the Promised Land. This was a man absolutely convinced that God holds the future, and that there is no power so great that it can stop God's promises from being fulfilled. Joseph lived out that belief in his life, and he believed it would continue to be true after his death.

There are many moments of faith which Joseph could have been remembered for – sticking to God through his trials, boldly interpreting dreams, managing a prosperous country – and yet, it's his faith for the future for which he is commended. Throughout the course of Hebrews 11, we've seen many interesting elements of faith, from the importance of worship and walking with God, to being willing to step into the unknown and take action obediently to follow after our Father in heaven. This principle is as important as any of them. Faith is believing in the promise, even if you don't see it realised in your lifetime. Faith is trusting God entirely for the future in the years we have on this earth, but also after we are gone. It is a great relief to know God will not abandon that ministry, that work, that family member, simply because we are not involved or around any more. He cares more for those precious things than even we do; we don't need to worry about letting go.

This is an incredibly important truth to grasp, because worries for our future can cripple our effectiveness here and now, in the present. I can't tell you how many times I have sat at my computer, ready to write, and stared for hours at a blank screen. When I really dig down into that lack of productivity, it is so often related to fear for the future. I question whether people will enjoy what I'm writing, whether my projects will fail or, perhaps even more terrifying, whether they will succeed, and life as I know it will change.

I am fully convinced God has a plan and a purpose for each of us,[10] that we are created anew in Christ Jesus for good works, which God has prepared for us to do.[11] Imagine if we lived as if we believed that, and didn't let worry stop us stepping into the promises he has for us. Imagine what we could achieve, if we didn't allow doubts to tell us there was no point, that God doesn't care, that it will all fall apart one day anyway. What if we could trust the Alpha and Omega, the God who was there at the beginning and who will be there at the end, the God who knows us, who knows our potential, who created us for a future greater than anything we could ever imagine?

I wonder how the story of Israel would have turned out if Joseph had spent those thirteen years refusing to do anything because it didn't look like the future he'd envisioned. In that time of darkness, he served God wholeheartedly, trusting God to work out the future details, not complaining and moaning and muttering about how the dream could never come to pass now. It was through those thirteen years, managing Potiphar's household and the prison, that Joseph learnt the skills he would need to manage a kingdom. We have no idea what God may be teaching us in this present moment which we will need for the future promise.

We can learn from Joseph's example to put this exceedingly important idea into practice. Throughout this man's days, we see God delivering him time after time, sparing his life and eventually bringing him into a position of power, the fulfilment of a distant dream. Joseph could look back on his life and see God's faithfulness. If you want to have faith for your future, begin by remembering God's hand on your past. Look back on your life, think of those times God moved on your behalf, when dreams were fulfilled, when things worked out in miraculous ways. The next time I move across a continent, I will remember how the road before me was so perfectly paved to get me to Liberia, even through the madness of the moment. I can trust God with any future move, knowing he so wonderfully orchestrated things for the previous one.

Joseph was 110 when he died. He was seventeen (or thereabouts) when he was taken to Egypt. The vast majority of his life was lived in a foreign land, away from the place promised to the patriarchs, his ancestors. It would have been easy to believe the Israelites were simply meant to stay in Egypt, to forget the Promised Land, but Joseph chose to trust in the word over the world. It was not the first time he'd done so. When he shared his dreams as a teenager, he was mocked for it, told he was crazy, but he knew they were a promise from God to stand on. The world will tell you, over and over, that God's promises will fail, that you should give up. Don't listen. Stand on the word. Our future is secured by God; that's all we need to know.

Finally, it's important to remember not to become complacent, particularly when life feels comfortable. It would have been so easy for Joseph to forget the future promises of God, enjoying life in his palace with his wife and his children. Rather than forgetting, Joseph planned for that future, providing instructions for the Israelites regarding his body. Many years before Joseph's time, God told Abraham his descendants would reside in a foreign land where they would be enslaved and mistreated for 400 years. Joseph's absolute certainty the Israelites would return to their Promised Land may well have been a comfort for his descendants throughout that time. Having faith for the future is an encouragement to us, absolutely, but it can also encourage those around us, spurring them on to trust in our faithful God and his wonderful promises.

It is incredible that God is a part of our entire story, our past, our present and our future. We can entrust him with whatever will come, and find contentment and peace here and now, whatever we may face, knowing God holds our future.

Questions for Further Study

Background reading:

Hebrews 11:22
Genesis 50:22-26

There is a lot more to Joseph's life than the passage in Genesis 50 which relates to Hebrews 11. If you want to examine the life of Joseph in greater depth, read Genesis 37 – 50.

What do we know about Joseph? What was his life like?

Why is Joseph remembered as a man of faith in Hebrews 11?

Why was this the most significant thing he did by faith?

Do you find it hard to have faith about your future? Why/why not?

What do these verses tell us about our future?

Jeremiah 29:11	
Revelation 21:3-4	
James 4:13-15	
1 Corinthians 2:9	
Romans 8:18	

Do any of these verses stand out to you? Why?

If we are fully entrusting our future to God, does that mean we shouldn't make plans for it?

Read Acts 7:9-10.

This very brief summary of Joseph's life suggests things weren't always easy for him. Why might what he went through have helped him to keep walking with God?

Can you remember a time when God came through for you? How does this help you believe in his promises for your future?

Read Genesis 39:5, Genesis 39:20-23 and Genesis 41:15-16.

What was Joseph's relationship with God like throughout this time of his life?

Why is relationship with God so important if we are to keep having faith for our future?

Contrast those verses with a passage from earlier in Joseph's life, in Genesis 37:2-8. **What was Joseph like as a teenager?**

Why might the time of hardship in Egypt have been important for him, and for God's purpose in saving the nation of Israel from the famine to come?

Sometimes God needs to work on our characters before he can bring about his purpose in our lives. John 15:2 talks about the great gardener pruning us so we can bear more fruit, a potentially painful process. **How can we keep hold of God's promises in those times?**

Read Exodus 13:19 and Joshua 24:32.

What is the significance of these verses?

Joseph's faith for the future deliverance of Israel must have been an encouragement to the people, who hadn't forgotten his instruction in their hundreds of years in Egypt. **How can we encourage those around us in this way?**

Joseph faced a tough time through a long part of his life. Instead of drawing closer to the dream he was holding on to, it must have felt like he was getting further from it. He is a wonderful example of faith, because through it all he remembered his God and maintained his faith for the future. At the very end of his days, he was still excited about what God was going to do. It can be easy for us to get caught up in worrying about the future, instead of trusting that God will bring all things together for our good, especially when God's promises seem to be contradicted by the evidence of our eyes. Whether you have an idea of what the future will hold or no clue whatsoever, keep trusting it to God, knowing he is in control.

MOSES' PARENTS
FAITH IN THE DARKEST DAYS

'If God is so good, why do bad things happen?'

I'm sure you've heard that question at some point in your life, or one like it. Perhaps it's something you've found yourself asking, from time to time. You certainly wouldn't be alone; it's one I find particularly difficult to answer. I know all the usual arguments: the concept of our free will, which we as humanity so often use to abuse each other, the fact we live in a fallen and sinful world. Those arguments can make total sense, until you look on the pain and suffering of a person, even a believer in God, and feel your heart breaking for them, wondering why God wouldn't simply step into the scene and turn it all around. The arguments make sense, until you find yourself faced with a situation that feels beyond you, impossible to bear, and you don't know what to do.

It's in those darkest days of our lives that our faith can carry us through. God absolutely has the power the turn our situations around, but sometimes, even if we don't understand why right now, he allows us to go through difficulties and pain.

I imagine that the parents of Moses might have been asking questions like this themselves. It's been years now, decades, since the days of Joseph and his favour with the Pharaoh of Egypt. We've left the book of Genesis behind and entered into Exodus, and with it, we find the people of God in a dire situation.

> *So they put slave masters over them to oppress them with forced labour, and they built Pithom and Rameses as store cities for Pharaoh. But the more they were oppressed, the more they multiplied and spread; so the Egyptians came to dread the Israelites and worked them ruthlessly. They made their lives bitter with harsh labour in brick and mortar and with all kinds of work in the fields; in all their harsh labour the Egyptians worked them ruthlessly.*
>
> **-Exodus 1:11-14-**

Amram and Jochebed, Moses' parents, are born into this environment. They grow up as slaves, in bondage to a ruthless Pharaoh who is so terrified of the populous Israelite people that his plan is to essentially work them to death.

Imagine for a moment what life must have been like for this couple. I can picture them up at the crack of dawn, Jochebed treating the raw and open sores on the back of her husband, from the last time the overseer was a bit too zealous with his whip when Amram was slow moving bricks from place to place. It must have been easy to imagine that God had well and truly abandoned them; his promises to Abraham and Isaac and Jacob were nothing but a distant dream, never to come to pass. They clung to the thought that Joseph expected his people to be able to move his bones back to the Promised Land one day, but couldn't see how it would ever happen. The days would have been long and hard, and they would collapse into their tiny hut each night exhausted and broken, tears filling their eyes as the days of their lives spanned into a horizon of misery before them.

Moses' parents were living in dark days.

As if that wasn't bad enough, Jochebed wakes up one day and realises her fears have come to pass; she's pregnant again. With a mixture of joy and absolute horror, she shares the news with Amram. They stare into the distance, wondering what this means. Should the child be born at all, amid the harsh labour and the bitterness of their existence (I can't imagine the Egyptians offered the best maternity leave to the Israelites), then the baby would be born to a life of slavery, moving from misery to misery with no hope of finding freedom. And what's more, if the baby were a boy, he would only make it to that kind of a life if he could somehow survive the king's edict:

> *Then Pharaoh gave this order to all his people: "Every Hebrew boy that is born you must throw into the Nile."*
>
> **-Exodus 1:15-16-**

It's easy to skip past this little part of the story as we read the Bible, moving from Joseph's interesting tale into the dramatic plagues and the exodus of the Israelites. Amram and Jochebed only appear in a few verses of the Bible; they're bit players, not main characters. I know it well; I was cast as Jochebed in a musical school production entitled 'Out of Egypt' as a ten or eleven-year-old. I enjoyed my one solo, but always felt a bit hard done to, not being able to show off my wonderful acting ability in more than one scene.

When you really stop and think about it, though, these two characters had a vital role to play, and are an incredible example to us today. In those darkest of days, where deliverance for the Israelites seemed an impossible dream, where daily pain and hardship and suffering was the reality, this couple stood fast in their faith.

> *By faith Moses' parents hid him for three months after he was born, because they saw he was no ordinary child, and they were not afraid of the king's edict.*
>
> **-Hebrews 11:23-**

We know the story ends well. Moses' parents keep their baby concealed for three months, tensing at his every cry, every day fearing his discovery. When they realise they simply can't hide him any longer, Jochebed creates a special basket for him, crafted from papyrus and carefully coated with tar and pitch to make it waterproof. With a broken heart, she places this beautiful baby into the basket, perhaps kisses him on the forehead one final time, and floats him away down the river.

We know he was found by Pharaoh's daughter, and even raised by Jochebed for the first few years of his life, until he moved in with Pharaoh's daughter and became her son. We know that, but Jochebed didn't. All she knew was this was the only hope of giving her son a chance at survival, even if he would probably be found by patrolling Egyptian guards who would fulfil their instructions. It's hard to imagine how painful that moment must have been, as she returned to the house, tears blinding her, leaving another child, a daughter, to watch and see what would happen because she couldn't stand to see it for herself.

This is darkness at its deepest.

This is the kind of faith that moves mountains, and there are specific things we can learn from their example to help us activate our own faith, when we face those darkest of moments.

No matter what you may encounter in your life, good or bad, faith looks at a situation with different eyes, it sees things differently.

It would have been easy for Moses' parents to see the obvious, the difficulty they faced, the hopelessness of it all. Instead, they looked at their baby, and saw that he was no ordinary child.

Different translations of Hebrews 11 phrase it in other words, some specifying that Moses was an unusual child, or beautiful. In the Amplified Bible, we read that *they saw he was a beautiful and divinely favoured child.* By some God-given sense, these parents saw something special in their baby boy, something worth taking a chance on.

When we face hard times in our lives, it's all too easy to fix our gaze on our circumstances, on the nightmare unfolding around us. On the morning when Dave woke up with severe abdominal pain and I had to rush him to hospital for an emergency appendectomy, it would have been easy to focus on everything I had heard about medical care in Liberia, the problems with anaesthesia and sterilisation, the potential infections, the standards which aren't quite at the same level I was used to, coming from the UK.

It's a natural thing for us to do, tuning in to the worries and the concerns and everything that could go wrong. But faith sees things differently, and looking back I marvel at the peace I found, sitting in the small hospital garden, waiting with some dear friends for news from the surgery. It's not that I didn't feel worried, it's not that there wasn't confusion in my brain as to why God would have allowed this to happen, but faith showed me how every circumstance aligned perfectly to bring Dave the best possible care that day.

Amram and Jochebed weren't stupid. They knew what was going on, the risks, and what looked likely to happen. Instead of turning their gaze onto that trouble, they recognised the gift God had given them: their fine, beautiful, unusual, divinely favoured son.

We can do the same today. We can choose to look at the good there is in our lives, even when things are difficult. We can remember the incredible promises God has spoken over us in his word, and remember the wonderful future promised to us, living our lives here and now in view of eternity.

In the book of 2 Kings, we find the prophet, Elisha, surrounded by horses and chariots who have come to capture and potentially kill him. When his servant looks out on the armies, he comes to Elisha in a panic:

> *"Oh no, my lord! What shall we do?" the servant asked.*
>
> *"Don't be afraid," the prophet answered. "Those who are with us are more than those who are with them."*
>
> *And Elisha prayed, "Open his eyes, LORD, so that he may see." Then the LORD opened the servant's eyes, and he looked and saw the hills full of horses and chariots of fire all around Elisha.*
>
> **-2 Kings 6:15-17-**

The servant's eyes looked to the darkness, to the impossible situation, to the hopelessness of it all. He could see their defeat, their capture, and the imprisonment and possible death which would follow.

Elisha was a human man, and I'm sure those thoughts flickered through his mind as well, but his faith allowed him to see things differently. Yes, he saw the army, he saw the problem, but he also saw the armies of the Lord, much greater than anything on earth which could come against him.

Have you ever heard that expression, don't tell God how big your problems are, tell your problems how big your God is? It's a similar idea; there is nothing you can ever face which is bigger than God. Yes, you may have to go through trials from time to time, but faith can help you keep your gaze fixed on our wonderful Saviour. Faith can help you see things differently.

Faith can also cast out fear.

I am positive that Amram and Jochebed were afraid. Their son's life was at stake. Their own lives were in jeopardy for hiding this boy from Pharaoh's soldiers. Having faith doesn't mean we don't feel fear, but faith has the capacity to completely conquer it, and that's why Hebrews 11 can tell us that they were not afraid of the king's edict. It doesn't mean they were superhumans who had overcome the human impulse to worry. It means their faith was stronger than their fear.

It's how I was able to sit calmly in the hospital grounds, unsure what would happen in the next hour. It's how the apostle Paul was able to face death and still pen the beautiful letter of 2 Timothy to his protégé. It's how Christians around the world can cope when there is war and terror and disease and disaster, being a shining beacon of light and sharing the love of Jesus through those terrible times.

Fear has the potential to cripple our effectiveness here on earth. It will tell us there's nothing we can do, we should give up, curl up under the blankets in our bedrooms and never leave the house again. It is a powerful feeling. I believe even Jesus felt it in that garden, knowing the horror that was to come, praying for this cup of suffering to be taken from him. Luke's account of the moment describes Jesus as being in anguish, with sweat like drops of blood falling to the ground.[12]

The great news is that feeling fear doesn't mean we have failed. We don't need to feel guilty because we've been afraid, or are afraid right now. We can experience fear, yet not allow that fear to conquer us. There are so many wonderful passages in the Bible which can help that voice of fear to be silenced by the activation of our faith.

> *The LORD is with me; I will not be afraid. What can man do to me?*
>
> -Psalm 118:6-
>
> *I sought the LORD, and he answered me; he delivered me from all my fears.*
>
> -Psalm 34:4-
>
> *For I am the LORD your God who takes hold of your right hand and says to you, Do not fear; I will help you.*
>
> -Isaiah 41:13-

The list goes on and on. Find these verses, read them when fear creeps into your heart, memorise them to repeat in those moments where fear would dare try to stop you from walking in the purposes of God for your life. Then you, too, will be like Moses' parents, who were not afraid of something terrifying, because they knew their God was greater.

Faith helps us to see things differently, and it can conquer any fear. Faith can also embolden us to take action. If Amram and Jochebed had looked on their baby boy, noticed something special about him but done nothing, the story may have played out very differently. Sometimes we need to take action – against injustice, against sin and evil, against the enemy's schemes, against our own complacency.

If God is calling you to action, even in a situation which seems hopeless and desperate, you need to take that first step. You have no idea what your small effort may set in motion. It took eighty years for Moses to return to Egypt to be instrumental in freeing the Israelites from their slavery, but it was this one bold action of his parents which allowed it to happen. You may never see the full impact of those small steps of faith, those little actions that you take here on this earth, but that makes them no less important. We can trust and obey, leaving the future safely in God's hands.

On the face of it, Moses' parents didn't do anything monumental. They didn't perform miracles, weren't remembered as the father and mother of faith, didn't pray blessings that would span generations into their children. What they did was trust in God absolutely, in the very worst situation imaginable, and through it their action ultimately led to the deliverance of their people.

Activated faith will let you see your circumstances differently. It will help you to cast out that crippling fear, and to take action in whatever situation you may face, no matter how dark and hopeless it may seem.

Questions for Further Study

Background reading:

Hebrews 11:23
Exodus 1:1 – 2:10

What do we know about Moses' parents? (Check Exodus 6 for their genealogy)

Why were they commended for their faith?

What was so special about Moses? What did they see in him?

Read 2 Corinthians 5:7.

How can we open our spiritual eyes to see what God wants us to see in a situation?

How would our faith differ if we looked at our world through God's eyes?

Read Exodus 1:11-14.

What conditions were Moses' parents living in at the time of Moses' birth?

How might living as slaves have impacted their faith?

Read Isaiah 43:2.

Note that this passage doesn't say *if* you pass through the waters, I will be with you, but when. We are not promised an easy life here on earth. **How can we keep our faith strong in the hardest and darkest moments of our lives?**

Hebrews 11:23 tells us Moses' parents were not afraid of the king's edict, even though their action could have put their own lives at risk. **What does this tell us about their faith?**

Are we more concerned with our own safety than what God is asking us to do?

_____

_____

_____

Have you ever failed to act on something God had called you to do because of fear?

_____

_____

_____

What do these verses tell us about fear and faith?

2 Timothy 1:7	
Philippians 4:6	
Psalm 118:6-7	
Deuteronomy 31:6	
Proverbs 29:25	

Does anything stand out to you from these verses? Why?

Read Romans 13:1.

The step of faith Moses' parents made meant breaking the law, but we are instructed in the Bible to be subject to the governing authorities. **What happens when our faith is at odds with the laws of the country we live in?**

As Christians, to what level should we be prepared to stand against injustice?

Look at Hebrews 11:23 again. What action did Moses' parents take?

Read James 2:14-17.

What does this passage tell us about faith?

What practical actions can we take alongside our faith?

Moses' parents lived in a difficult time in Israel's history. Living as slaves, they must surely have had many days without hope that their situation would ever change. Despite their position though, they continued to have faith, seeing something special in their child and taking action to save him, even though it could have had grave consequences. In our darkest days, in those moments where we struggle to see God and when we don't understand why he would be allowing our circumstances, we can still have faith, believing in his promises and trusting him in those small actions we can take.

MOSES

THE COMFORT OF FAITH

I am a creature of comfort. Take me out into the wilds of the world, that's fine, as long as I have a comfortable bed to return to at night. If it's a choice between camping and a nice, cosy hotel, I'd take the hotel any day.

I think all of us enjoy some measure of comfort. 'A state of physical ease and freedom from pain or constraint,' says one dictionary definition. That sounds very nice to me. The opposite – discomfort, a state without physical ease, with pain and constraint – sounds significantly less pleasant.

As an aviation mission, most of MAF's maintenance facilities are found within cities or major hubs, close to airports; we are certainly not living in mud huts in tiny villages in the middle of the African plains. We have electricity and running water (most of the time). And yet, there are comforts we've had to sacrifice. Living for four years in Uganda meant living for four years without any semblance of a good, strong cheddar cheese, for example. Our time in Liberia has been punctuated with prolonged water outages, which always seem to happen the moment you've put a load of washing in the machine, or started preparing some raw meat for dinner and need to wash your hands.

Those discomforts, however, are nothing compared with what our next character faced.

After his first few years with his mother, presumably once he was weaned, Moses grew up as the son of Pharaoh's daughter. In other words, he was known as the grandson of Pharaoh, one of the most powerful and wealthiest rulers in the entire world at that time. He grew up with wealth and privilege, with access to the best education available. He probably lived in some kind of palace, draped in opulence and splendour, with servants to care for his every need and whim. Chances are, the Pharaoh may have had many concubines and therefore many children; we're not entirely sure how close Moses may have been to that direct royal line of succession, but it is entirely possible he would have known the man who would be the Pharaoh when he would return to the country, many years later.

All in all, Moses was living a life of luxury. It would have been very easy for him to remain in that place, free from worries, free from physical distress and pain. But he chose a different path, as Hebrews 11 tells us:

> *By faith Moses, when he had grown up, refused to be known as the son of Pharaoh's daughter. He chose to be mistreated along with the people of God rather than to enjoy the fleeting pleasures of sin. He regarded disgrace for the sake of Christ as of greater value than the treasures of Egypt, because he was looking ahead to his reward. By faith he left Egypt, not fearing the king's anger; he persevered because he saw him who is invisible. By faith he kept the Passover and the application of blood, so that the destroyer of the firstborn would not touch the firstborn of Israel..*
>
> -Hebrews 11:24-28-

If I was writing about Moses' life of faith, I would probably choose different moments. I would talk about his standing against Pharaoh, calling down plagues onto the land of Egypt. I would talk about his leading a bunch of complaining Israelites through the desert for forty years. I would talk about him ascending into a mountain covered by the cloud of the literal presence of God, and surviving the experience!

This record of faith doesn't include those big moments, however. Some are alluded to, as the account speaks of the Passover, the moment of that final plague against the Egyptians when the firstborn of all families in the land would be killed, aside from the Israelites, but the bulk of Moses' faith journey in this record happens long before that moment.

If you were making a movie based on the life of Moses from this section of Hebrews 11, you might call it *Moses: The Origin Story*. It takes us back to that moment when Moses chose to leave the land of Egypt, to forego luxury to live as a shepherd in the wilderness for forty years, a profession which was detestable to the Egyptian people, as Joseph had explained to his brothers on their arrival in that country.[13] Not only did Moses have to say farewell to the life of luxury he was used to, but he was forced to become the lowest of the low, a prejudice which would surely have been in mind when he first started to watch the flocks of his father-in-law, Jethro, in the land of Midian.

This suggests that there is an important lesson for us here regarding comfort.

I'm confident that anyone with faith in Christ Jesus knows what a comfort that very real relationship with God can bring us. I can remember many moments in my life when I have questioned how people could possibly cope without the assurance of faith. When hard times hit, we can reach for the Bible and remind ourselves again that God is with us. We can spend time in prayer, and access that peace which passes understanding, even when we don't necessarily understand why we're going through the situation in which we find ourselves.

We know, with that wonderful gift of hindsight, that Moses will go on to have an incredible relationship with God, something which was undoubtedly a source of comfort to him. In order to get to that place, however, Moses needed to let go of some of the earthly comforts he had come to know. Sometimes, we can find ourselves in the same position.

This raises some interesting questions. If we wish to be people living lives of activated faith, do we need to give up all worldly comforts? Live in a cell in a monastery? Give away all of our possessions? Do we need to be living in constant disgrace for the sake of Christ? What does Moses' commendation of faith mean for us today?

Considering this passage in Hebrews 11 can help us to work that out.

I believe that Moses always had the capacity to be a great leader, but he had some growing up to do first.

> *By faith Moses, when he had grown up, refused to be known as the son of Pharaoh's daughter.*
>
> **-Hebrews 11:24-**

It's easy to read this passage and think that Moses was perhaps in his twenties when he made this choice, but he was forty years old. I expect we would have considered him to be 'grown up' long before that age, but in our lives there is both a physical growing up and a spiritual growing up. It took until Moses was forty for him to take a stroll to see his own people suffering, but surely he must have known of their slavery before then. He must have heard of their plight; perhaps he had been told the story of his own rescue, saved from the king's edict which would have had every baby boy among the Israelites slaughtered. Why did it take Moses so very long to do anything? We don't know. Perhaps he was simply enjoying his life and the luxuries of Egypt. Perhaps he didn't recognise how bad it was. Perhaps he wasn't willing to intervene until this point, fearing what might happen to him.

Whatever the reason, Moses had a bit of growing up to do to get to where he needed to be. The same is true for us. The Bible repeatedly tells us of the importance of growing and maturing as Christians.

> *Therefore let us move beyond the elementary teachings about Christ and be taken forward to maturity.*
> **-Hebrews 6:1a-**
>
> *Then we will no longer be infants, tossed back and forth by the waves, and blown here and there by every wind of teaching and by the cunning and craftiness of people in their deceitful scheming. Instead, speaking the truth in love, we will grow to become in every respect the mature body of him who is the head, that is, Christ.*
> **-Ephesians 4:14-15-**

Our Christian walk is a journey towards the maturity we will only fully attain when we reach heaven, but it's a process we are all undertaking here and now. As we do grow up spiritually, we may well start to notice things in our lives which aren't quite right, the comforts we have enjoyed which are not helping us to live the life God has called us to. Moses realised that being known as the son of Pharaoh's daughter might have looked and felt good on the outside, but it was not something which would help him live in the fullness of God's purposes for his life.

Not all things which bring us comfort are bad. I don't believe there's anything wrong with a good mattress or the occasional piece of cheese, but anything which might lead us further from God needs consideration. Anything we might begin to rely on more than him. Anything that stops us living in the fullness of the life won for us at the cross. And especially, anything which leads us towards sin.

> *He chose to be mistreated along with the people of God rather than to enjoy the fleeting pleasures of sin.*
>
> **-Hebrews 11:25-**

For Moses, the influences of Egypt luring him away from God may have been obvious. The Egyptians worshipped other gods. They held beliefs counter to those of the patriarchs, counter to what the Israelites knew of the one true God. The lines can be blurrier for us today, but there are as many idols in our world now as in the world Moses faced. There are as many temptations to seek comfort in, from the easy access to pornography, to the lure of wealth, to the endless desire for stuff, to tuning out the horror stories of suffering such as the modern-day slavery and human trafficking which exists in every country.

As Moses looked on and saw an Egyptian beating one of his own people, he made a decision. I'm sure part of his action was impulsive, and we know it wasn't exactly the right choice for him to make, committing murder in a misguided attempt to rescue his people. Even so, in that instant, Moses must have recognised that this action was the first step on the journey to turning away from the pleasures and the sin he had known. He chose to distance himself from the damage sin can cause in our lives, despite the extreme cost, the loss of his luxurious way of life.

We face similar choices today, perhaps in not quite such a dramatic way, but equally as important. This very day, you can choose whether you will follow the path of sin with its temporary pleasures, or take the harder path, which may appear less comfortable on the surface.

> *He regarded disgrace for the sake of Christ as of greater value than the treasures of Egypt, because he was looking ahead to his reward.*
>
> **-Hebrews 11:26-**

The treasures of Egypt were vast – unimaginable wealth, everything your earthly heart could desire – and yet those treasures can't hold a candle to the reward we have to come.

We know a lot more about this reward than Moses did. Most of the prophecies about Jesus would come many, many years after his time. Moses didn't have a handy Bible to reference, and he didn't have the Holy Spirit indwelling within him as comforter and advocate and guide. Despite that, he still trusted in the covenant God had made with Abraham, and confirmed with Isaac and Jacob. He trusted God had a plan for the future, a plan for an eternity of so much more than the fleeting pleasure we can find here and now. Moses set aside the treasures of Egypt, because he was looking forward.

It's all too easy for us to get caught up in looking at what's happening around us right now, at what feels good in this moment, but it is so important to keep an eternal focus. It's much easier to give up the things we treasure on earth, the things that are comfortable here and now, when we keep our eyes fixed on the wonder of all that is to come, a future of complete and perfect comfort, with no more death or mourning or crying or pain, a world made new. There is a reward coming. Don't miss out on the best in eternity because of the lure of a treasure you can only enjoy temporarily here on earth. As missionary and martyr, Jim Elliot famously said, 'He is no fool who gives what he cannot keep to gain what he cannot lose.'

> *By faith he left Egypt, not fearing the king's anger; he persevered because he saw him who is invisible.*
>
> **-Hebrews 11:27-**

Moses could put aside the comfort of this world, by keeping his focus on him who is invisible. He could persevere in the face of hardship and adversity, by seeing with his spiritual eyes.

I find this verse fascinating. If there is one person in the Bible who saw the visible God more than any other, it was Moses. He saw the burning bush. He asked to see the glory of God and watched as God passed by. God himself describes his interactions with Moses in this way:

> *With him I speak face to face, clearly and not in riddles; he sees the form of the LORD.*
>
> **-Numbers 12:8a-**

Moses would go on to see God in so many wonderful ways, but he is commended for seeing the invisible God. I often wonder, as I read through the Old Testament, how the Israelites could so easily go astray after seeing such a physical representation of God in the pillar of cloud and fire which accompanied them for forty years, but perhaps it is because all they could see was the visible, not the invisible.

One of Jesus' disciples found it hard to believe that Jesus had been raised from the dead. He determined he would only believe if he could put his hands into the wounds on Jesus' living body. Jesus, full of so much kindness and grace, allowed Thomas to see.

> *Then Jesus told him, "Because you have seen me, you have believed; blessed are those who have not seen and yet have believed."*
>
> **-John 20:29-**

Seeing and believing is all well and good, but believing without seeing is even better. Fixing our eyes on the invisible God rather than what is visible and tangible keeps our eyes fixed on the miracle worker, rather than the miracle. It keeps our eyes fixed on the ultimate comfort-bringer, rather than the temporary comfort of the here and now.

Moses' confidence in God was such that whether he could see God or not, he would persevere in his faith. He would still take the more difficult path. Whether there were visible miracles or not, he would choose to put his trust in the God he knew.

What an encouragement this is for us today. In those moments where we need to take the more difficult route, to forsake some earthly comfort, we know the comfort we can find in faith is worth the sacrifice, and is ultimately greater than any temporary gain we can find in this world.

We can follow Moses' example in our lives today, by ensuring we are maturing in our spiritual walk, going deeper into our relationship with God so that we can begin to see those areas in our lives where some correction may be needed. We can follow Moses' example in our lives today by making the choice to step away from the sin that so easily entangles and walking with God instead, by keeping our gaze fixed on eternity, knowing our reward is waiting for us. And finally, we can follow Moses' example in our lives today by trusting absolutely in the invisible God, believing he is working on our behalf, even if we can't see it with our physical eyes right now.

The comfort of faith is so much greater than the fleeting comforts of the world, and recognising that can help us rest in that blessed assurance all the more.

Questions for Further Study

Background reading:

Hebrews 11:24-28
Exodus 2:11-25
Exodus 12:1-30

Who was Moses? What do we know about this Bible character?

What did Moses do to be counted in the list of people of faith in Hebrews 11?

Why do you think this was significant?

Read Acts 7:20-29.

How old was Moses when he left Egypt?

Moses had lived as the son of Pharaoh's daughter for all of that time; why might this have made his decision to leave Egypt more difficult?

What were Moses' reasons for leaving Egypt?

Do you think Moses was following God's specific instruction in his actions at this time?

Moses left behind the comforts of being a part of the royal family of one of the richest nations in the world. Is a comfortable life a bad thing? Why/why not?

How can we distinguish between good comforts and those which distance us from God?

Can you think of any comforts in your life that might have too high a priority? Are they things that need changing?

What do the following verses tell us about comfort?

Psalm 23:4	
Psalm 119:76	
2 Corinthians 1:3-4	
Isaiah 51:12	
John 14:26*	

*Look at this verse in different translations if you have access to them – 'Advocate' has many meanings.

What do these verses, along with Moses' example, tell us about where we should find comfort in our lives?

Read Hebrews 11:27 and Exodus 2:14.

These two verses seem contradictory regarding how Moses was feeling – do you think he was afraid? Why?

Choosing the less comfortable path can sometimes seem scary. Consider Hebrews 11:24-27 again. What made Moses think this path was worth it?

How can we apply those lessons to our own lives?

Read Hebrews 11:28.

This verse talks about a different occasion to the rest of the verses about Moses. Why did Moses need faith to keep the first Passover?

180

The Passover refers to the event that allowed the Israelites to leave Egypt, just as Moses had done forty years before. How do you think that would have made Moses feel?

_____

_____

_____

The Passover is a wonderful picture of the sacrifice Jesus made to save our lives. I encourage you to take a moment here to thank God for the amazing comfort we have because he sent his Son to take our place on the cross.

In whatever situations we face in our lives, we have access to the comfort that comes through faith. Moses left behind the comforts this world tells us are incredibly important, and throughout his life he developed an incredible relationship with God. I'm sure the answer would not be in doubt if you asked him at the end of his life which comfort meant more. God might not be asking you to give up everything comfortable in your life, but it is still important to consider what is more important to us – our faith in the invisible God, or the things we have in front of us here and now.

THE ISRAELITES
FAITH IN THE BATTLE

Good versus evil. It's a classic trope in literature, a familiar story where the good guy goes up against the villain in a contest which may seem unwinnable. We cheer for the underdog, the hero, the David facing down his Goliath, and feel a sense of satisfaction when good triumphs over evil, and the day is won.

There's a reason we see this story echoing through our books and our movies and our television shows. It's because the battle of good and evil is a very real war, one that is being waged right now, even as you read these words.

It was the French philosopher, Charles Baudelaire, who first said, 'One of the artifices of Satan is, to induce men to believe that he does not exist.' Or, to put it in its more modern context, 'The greatest trick the Devil ever pulled was convincing the world he didn't exist.' As Christians today, it's all too easy to forget there is an enemy standing against us who, if he can't steal our salvation, will do all within his power to render us ineffective. He will throw doubts at us, knowing the areas in which we are weak, knowing the words that will make us pause and wonder if we're really right to put as much faith in God as we do. He will turn our attention to the waves that threaten to crash over us and away from Jesus, who stands above those waves, holding out his hand.

> *Be alert and of sober mind. Your enemy the devil prowls around like a roaring lion looking for someone to devour.*
>
> **-1 Peter 5:8-**

We are at war.

But the great news? We are on the winning side, and with activated faith we can take our stand against the Devil's schemes.[14] As Peter goes on to say:

> *Resist him, standing firm in the faith, because you know that the family of believers throughout the world is undergoing the same kind of sufferings.*
>
> **-1 Peter 5:9-**

As we stand firm in our faith, we have the power to resist anything the Devil can throw at us. We will not be devoured. We will not be overcome. We will not be defeated. We have everything we need to stand strong, when we stand firm in our faith.

Throughout the course of this book, we've realised the importance of faith, from our everyday walk with God, choosing to allow him to be a part of our normal routines, to the ark-building faith of those moments when we're asked to step into something new and scary. From the moment of trial and testing, to the moment of hanging on through the darkest and most desperate moments. We need faith in each and every aspect of our lives, including the battles.

In Paul's letter to the Ephesians, there's a beautiful passage about the armour of God. The contents of those few verses are subject enough for an entire book, but I love this assurance of how powerful our faith is in this battle we face:

> *In addition to all this, take up the shield of faith, with which you can extinguish all the flaming arrows of the evil one.*
>
> **-Ephesians 6:16-**

Fire arrows weren't quite as powerful a force as we are led to believe from watching modern movies. That moment where Robin Hood's woodland hideout is destroyed by the Sheriff of Nottingham's men shooting fire arrows at it would likely not have happened. The Prince of Thieves and his merry men could have stayed safely on their higher ground, gradually peppering the enemy with their own arrows (it wouldn't have made quite as dramatic a scene though!). The vast majority of flaming darts would be extinguished as they flew through the air. However, there is some evidence to suggest the Romans engineered a solution for this, using reeds or bamboo filled with a flammable liquid, which would spill on the target, setting them alight on contact. It's not a particularly pleasant thought! Even if the flaming arrow or dart were to miss you, it would be an enormous distraction in the battle; suddenly you have flames to deal with, turning your attention away from the fight.

I always picture Paul looking out on his Roman guards as he penned this particular segment of the book of Ephesians from house arrest in Rome. Could he see a soldier, holding that iconic door-shaped shield? A shield large enough to hide behind. A shield made of charred wood and coated in leather, one that could be soaked with water before a battle, ready to extinguish any kind of fiery dart. A shield which, when interlocked with the shields of your brothers and sisters in arms, could form a mighty tortoise, a near impenetrable wall, protecting you from all incoming attacks.

This is what faith is for us believers today. When the enemy seeks to distract you from your purpose on this earth, faith is your shield. But as you'll note from Paul's writing, you need to take it up. It's all too easy to leave that shield on the ground, deactivated, leaving you wide open to attack. It's your choice, whether you will enter each new day equipped for battle, faith activated, or not.

We are not the first people to face a fight in our lives. Hebrews 11 introduces us to two separate instances where the Israelite people faced armies, and through their examples, we can learn more about what it means to pick up that shield of faith to face our battles today.

> *By faith the people passed through the Red Sea as on dry land; but when the Egyptians tried to do so, they were drowned.*
>
> *By faith the walls of Jericho fell, after the army had marched around them for seven days.*
>
> **-Hebrews 11:29-30-**

These two very different situations faced by the Israelite people are amazing examples of the victory we can see when we put our trust in God during the battle.

The first story takes us back to Moses, after he has led the people out of their enslavement in Egypt. The Israelites have only recently witnessed ten plagues decimating the nation which held them captive, the mighty hand of God at work. Now they find themselves facing the Red Sea, an impassable barrier, with the fearsome army of Egypt approaching their rear. The dust from Egypt's chariots is whipped into the air and, as the Israelites look back, they know they are trapped. They begin to panic, but then the Red Sea is parted before their very eyes and they walk to safety on dry land.

The second story jumps forward in time by forty years or so. The Israelites have wandered in the desert for decades, waiting for the generation who doubted God's promises to them to die off. Now they have crossed the Jordan river in an equally miraculous fashion, and are presented with an enormous city to conquer; their first conflict in the land of their promise. In order to see God's promises to Abraham, Isaac and Jacob fulfilled, they would have to fight.

We face battles in our lives every day, but from time to time there are specific moments when things feel particularly difficult and we genuinely feel under attack. We can feel as though we are trapped with the Red Sea in front and a hostile force behind, not knowing how to act, not knowing what to do, not understanding how God could possibly make a way in that situation. I think it's very common for us to respond a bit like the Israelites in those moments. What's going on here, God? Why have you brought me to this place? Why aren't you doing anything to stop this from happening? Let me go back to the way things were; they weren't perfect, but at least they were familiar.

The terrified Israelites cry out to the Lord and to Moses, looking like anything other than a people of faith. The answer Moses gives them is beautiful:

> "Do not be afraid. Stand firm and you will see the deliverance the LORD will bring you today. The Egyptians you see today you will never see again. The LORD will fight for you; you need only to be still."
>
> **-Exodus 14:13-14-**

What a reassurance those words must have been. The Lord, the same Lord who brought you to this place against impossible odds, that Lord is the one who is going to fight for you. You don't need to do anything, simply be still and watch God himself move on your behalf to bring you deliverance. How similar those words sound to Paul's in the book of Ephesians:

> *Therefore put on the full armour of God, so that when the day of evil comes, you may be able to stand your ground, and after you have done everything, to stand.*
>
> **-Ephesians 6:13-**

Stand firm. Stand your ground. After everything, no matter what happens, continue to stand.

This is a very different situation to that which we find across a desert and forty years' distance, as the people face down an enormous and powerful city. This time they're not told to stand, to be still – quite the opposite. The Israelites are told to march around the city of Jericho each day for six days as the priests blow on their trumpets. On the seventh day they must take a long hike, walking around the city seven times, carrying any weapons and armour they possessed, and let forth a deafening shout which would normally be reserved for after the battle as a declaration of victory.

In both of these situations, we see God's powerful hand at work, and yet they are very different. We have a tendency to imagine that God will work in the same way he has always worked, but in reality, his methods change. Could God have brought down the walls of Jericho if the people had stood firm and been still and waited to see him move? Of course he could! But in this particular battle, the Israelites were to be actively involved in taking the ground they had been promised.

In both of these situations, the people needed faith. The people fleeing from the armies of Egypt needed faith to believe the wall of water wouldn't crash down on them, killing them all. It must have taken an incredible amount of trust in God to take those first steps, watching the walls of water on either side, to believe God could hold up the Egyptians long enough for a couple of million people to cross to the other side. The Israelite army needed faith to believe that God would make a way into the city, that they could succeed in combat against the armed forces found within, after walking for hours and with limited experience in a fight.

In any situation we find ourselves in, now or in the future, on any battleground, we can have faith that God will be right there with us, regardless of how he chooses to work. And even when we wobble and doubt, we can pick that shield of faith up again, and honestly say to God that we may feel scared, we may feel uncertain, but we believe that he can win the fight for us.

The Israelites had equal cause to feel fear and panic in the second story, and yet we don't read of that reaction as they look on the great city of Jericho. And yet, despite the wavering of the first group, the Israelites are commended for their faith in both stories. I find that greatly encouraging. Just as Sarah and Abraham found it hard to believe for their promise, and yet still received it, God sees our moments of doubt, and yet continues to stand by us. In both of these stories, the Israelites faced a situation that was beyond their own strength to handle, yet God could see their hearts. He knew their limits and their strengths, and he provided a way through to match.

As we get better at living lives of faith, we may find ourselves invited to join the battle as a more active participant, to take ground back from the enemy. There will be moments in your life when it's all you can do to hunker down behind that shield of faith and let it protect you from the enemy's assault, and there will be moments when God will call you to march forward into enemy territory, to pray ferociously for those people he has stolen, to stand against injustice and corruption, to use your time and gifts and talents to reach out to the lost. The battle belongs to the Lord, but there are times when we will be called to action within it. In either instance, when the battle is brought to us, or when we bring the battle to the enemy, we can find reassurance in the knowledge that whatever we are facing, we can overcome.

As the inspirational author and artist Joni Eareckson Tada once said, 'This is the only time in history when I get to fight for God. This is the only part of my eternal story when I am actually in the battle. Once I die, I'll be in celebration mode in a glorified body in a whole different set of circumstances. But this is my limited window of opportunity, and I'm going to fight the good fight for all I'm worth.'

This may sound a little intimidating, but in reality it is incredibly exciting. God is inviting us to be a part of his work here on earth, and that may sometimes require a Jericho moment. But we get to enter those fights with full confidence of God's victory. Before the Israelite army had taken a single step around the city of Jericho, God told Joshua the outcome:

> *Then the LORD said to Joshua, "See, I have delivered Jericho into your hands, along with its king and its fighting men."*
> **-Joshua 6:2-**

And this is what God tells us, today:

> *Resist the devil, and he will flee from you.*
> **-James 4:7-**
>
> *For every child of God defeats this evil world, and we achieve this victory through our faith.*
> **-1 John 5:4-**
>
> *If God is for us, who can be against us?*
> **-Romans 8:31-**
>
> *Thanks be to God! He gives us the victory through our Lord Jesus Christ.*
> **-1 Corinthians 15:57-**

We do not need to fight alone. As the young David approached the giant, Goliath, it must have looked as though he was very much alone, and yet he knew this truth well:

> *"All those gathered here will know that it is not by sword or spear that the LORD saves; for the battle is the LORD's, and he will give all of you into our hands."*
> **-1 Samuel 17:47-**

This battle we are in is the Lord's, not our own. He is with us in it.

In both of the fights the Israelites faced, we see God entering into the lives of his people to help them in the battle. He defied the laws of physics, holding up an ocean to allow his people to cross on dry ground. He caused the thick walls of a city to crash down and be reduced to a dust so fine that an army could charge in with nothing hampering them.

Today, God enters into the lives of his people, providing them with the protection and weapons they need to stand against the enemy and to do battle. As we take up our shield of faith, our helmet of salvation, our belt of truth, our breastplate of righteousness, our shoes of peace, and the sword of the Spirit, the word of God, we can take our stand against any of the Devil's schemes. We can stand firm, trusting in God and the victory which was won on a wooden cross.

Questions for Further Study

Background reading:

Hebrews 11:29-30
Exodus 14
Joshua 6:1-21

Summarise the situations in Exodus 14 and Joshua 6:1-21.

Why did the Israelites need faith in these battles?

Read Exodus 14:10-12.

What is the reaction of the Israelites when the Egyptian army appears?

Compare this with the record in Hebrews 11:29. Why are the Israelites commended for having faith in this situation, considering their first reaction?

What can we learn from this in those times where we find our own faith struggling?

How was the reaction of the Israelites different at Jericho compared with at the Red Sea?

Why do you think this might have been the case when both situations needed a lot of faith?

Read Exodus 14:13-14.

What were the Israelites instructed to do?

What does it mean for us to stand firm to see the Lord fighting for us? How can we do that?

Read Joshua 6:2-5.

What were the Israelites instructed to do now?

These instructions are much more active than those for the people waiting by the Red Sea. Why do you think this is?

What are we called to fight against in our lives today?

Are we supposed to have an active or a passive role in spiritual warfare?

Why do we need faith in the battle we face against the Devil?

Consider the following verses. What do they tell us about the war we're part of?

2 Corinthians 10:3-4	
Ephesians 6:11-12	
Colossians 2:15	
1 Timothy 6:12	
1 Peter 5:8-9	
Psalm 18:32-35	

Do these verses help you to have faith for any battles you might be facing? Why/why not?

In both fights the Israelites faced, God worked in a miraculous way. What does this tell us?

Should we expect to see miracles as we enter the fight? Do we?

It is very encouraging to see how God stepped in to fight for the Israelite people. The involvement of the Israelites was different each time, but without fail, God came through for his people. Jesus has won the ultimate victory for us already, and though the Bible is clear that we are called to fight in this spiritual battle and that it won't always be easy, we do it with an assurance that we are on the winning team. Remembering that is the best way to keep our faith activated, through anything the enemy might throw at us.

RAHAB
SAVED THROUGH FAITH

There will be multiple moments in this day alone in which you will put your faith in something to save you.

It could be the brakes of your car; as you jump behind the wheel and drive to your destination, you trust that your vehicle will respond when you stamp on the brake pedal. It could be the chair you're sitting on as you read this book. You trust that it won't collapse beneath you as you put your weight on it, causing you to bang your head as you fall over. It could be as simple as trusting that the walls of your house aren't about to come crashing down. You put trust in the architect and the builder of your home, even if you never consciously think about them.

Faith is a part of everyday life. We put our trust in doctors, in mechanics, in firefighters, and we believe those people will do all they can to save us, not hurt us. I'm not sure we would get much enjoyment out of life if we believed every person was always out to get us, and worried constantly about death lurking behind each corner.

And yet, people can let us down. People can make mistakes. I will never forget the day when Dave phoned me from the side of a motorway in England after one of the wheels had all but fallen off our car as he was driving along at seventy miles per hour. Did I believe the mechanic had over-tightened the bolts deliberately to harm us? Of course not! But accidents can happen.

How wonderful, therefore, that we can put our faith in the one who will never make a mistake, who will never let us down, and who assures us of our absolute salvation.

> *For it is by grace you have been saved, through faith—and this is not from yourselves, it is the gift of God—not by works, so that no one can boast.*
>
> **-Ephesians 2:8-9-**

It is because of God's great love for us that he sent his one and only son, not to condemn the world, but to save the world through him, that whoever believes in him would not perish, but have eternal life.[15] What an incredible gift! It is only through grace that we are saved. It is through the sacrifice of Jesus on a cross that we get to enjoy a marvellous eternity.

Our faith does play a part, however; we are saved through faith. Our faith is our confession that we do believe in him, that it is only through him that we can be made righteous and whole. After all, all of us have sinned and fall short of the glory of God.[16]

The final character we meet in the chapter of Hebrews 11 was certainly a person who had fallen short. In almost every reference to her in the Bible, she is introduced as 'the prostitute Rahab'. That's not something done to disparage her, but rather to remind us that there is no one too broken, too tarnished, too sinful to receive God's saving grace.

> *By faith the prostitute Rahab, because she welcomed the spies, was not killed with those who were disobedient.*
>
> **-Hebrews 11:31-**

We've already visited this scene, from the perspective of the Israelites marching around the walls of Jericho, but now we're taken inside the city, to a woman who received salvation from certain death for herself and her family. Although Rahab welcomed the spies, it was not that action which saved her. It was by faith that she, and those nearest and dearest to her, escaped destruction.

Rahab goes on to be accepted by the people of Israel. She makes a life with them, and marries into God's chosen people, as we discover in the book of Matthew:

> *Salmon the father of Boaz, whose mother was Rahab,*
> *Boaz the father of Obed, whose mother was Ruth,*
> *Obed the father of Jesse,*
> *and Jesse the father of King David..*
>
> **-Matthew 15:6-**

A gentile prostitute is included in the genealogy of Christ Jesus. A gentile prostitute was the great-great grandmother of King David. There's some conjecture that Salmon, Rahab's husband, could have been one of the two spies she welcomed and concealed in the city of Jericho. Not only was she saved through faith, but her faith led her to a life that was exponentially better than she could have dreamt of. A life that would have an impact reaching far beyond anything she could have ever expected. A life in which she would come to know more of the God of Israel, and to follow after him, raising a godly son whom we learn more of in the book of Ruth.

Rahab's faith resulted in her slate being wiped clean. The same is true of us, when we declare with our mouths that Jesus is Lord, and believe in our hearts that God raised him from the dead.[17]

> *"Everyone who calls on the name of the Lord will be saved."*
>
> **-Romans 10:13-**

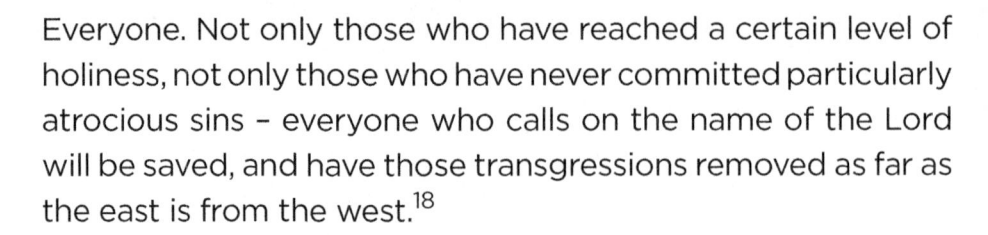

Everyone. Not only those who have reached a certain level of holiness, not only those who have never committed particularly atrocious sins – everyone who calls on the name of the Lord will be saved, and have those transgressions removed as far as the east is from the west.[18]

These verses are important to remember, no matter how long you may have been a Christian. They are a wonderful reminder that it is only through the work of Jesus that we can stand today, assured of our salvation. In taking time to remember that glorious gift, we can feel our faith begin to stir anew. The faith through which we have been saved, the faith that first brought us into a right relationship with God, can spur us on to amazing works of faith throughout our lives. If you want the faith of Noah, to build your ark, the faith of Abraham, to stand against the test, the faith of Moses' parents, to keep the faith in a dark and difficult situation, begin by remembering your salvation. You have all the faith you need today, and you can activate it by remembering the incredible gift Jesus offered us so freely.

And if you've never made that decision, there's no better time than now to call on the name of the Lord and begin your adventure in faith today.

Let's put ourselves in the place of Rahab. Rumours are flying around the city, of this people called the Israelites. There are many of them, millions, and stories are spreading about how they were able to leave the land of Egypt, decades ago, how God himself dried up the Red Sea and allowed his people to walk across on dry ground. You hear too about the people the Israelites have just defeated on the other side of the Jordan river, not that far away from Jericho, this city which has always seemed so safe with its high walls.

> *When we heard of it, our hearts melted in fear and everyone's courage failed because of you, for the LORD your God is God in heaven above and on the earth below.*
>
> **-Joshua 2:11-**

Rahab explains how her own heart melted in fear, along with everyone else in the city, as they heard these stories. She was terrified, she feared for her life, but in that moment, she recognised a startling truth: the Israelites weren't powerful because they were particularly fierce warriors or notably strong; they would overcome because they followed the God in heaven above and on the earth below.

In Hebrews 11 we're told Rahab was not killed with those who were disobedient, but some other translations specify that she was not killed with those who did not believe. The difference between this terrified woman and the rest of the terrified population was that she believed. She saw there was something real about this God, something different to the gods her own people followed. She realised this was the God she wanted to follow herself. It was that belief which distinguished her, and I very much doubt she had that moment of clarity as she invited the spies into her home. She must have been musing on those thoughts for some time; she had already established in her heart that this God was something particularly special.

A crucial part of faith is believing that God is who he says he is, that he will do what he says he will do. Do you truly believe that God is good? Do you believe he is mighty? Do you believe he is able to deliver you from whatever you may be facing right now? Do you believe what he says about you? That you are fearfully and wonderfully made, created for a purpose, made in the very image of God, a wholly new creation, more than a conqueror? I could go on and on. Rahab believed, and so can we.

With that belief burning in her heart, she was able to act.

Bringing two Israelite spies into her home could have cost Rahab significantly. The king of Jericho discovered where they were; if his men had found the spies hiding within, I don't think he would have had much sympathy for Rahab. Her life could have been on the line. She was willing to put herself in danger to welcome God's people.

James has much to say about faith and action in his book in the Bible:

> *You foolish person, do you want evidence that faith without deeds is useless?*
>
> **-James 2:20-**

He goes on to talk about Abraham, the father of faith, and how he was considered righteous because of his action, his willingness to offer his son Isaac on the altar.

> *You see that a person is considered righteous by what they do and not by faith alone.*
>
> **-James 2:24-**

James is not saying that we are saved by the things we do, but rather that our faith should prompt us into action, that action is the evidence of our faith. The big question is, if we're happy to sit and do nothing, is our faith genuine? Rahab could very easily have nodded pointedly at the piles of flax on her roof beneath which the spies were hiding when the king's men called. It would have been the easier option. She would have saved herself. But her belief in the God of these men, and in his saving power, led her to act.

> *In the same way, was not even Rahab the prostitute considered righteous for what she did when she gave lodging to the spies and sent them off in a different direction? As the body without the spirit is dead, so faith without deeds is dead.*
>
> -James 2:25-26-

If we are to be a people of faith we absolutely need to believe in God and his promises to us, but we also need to put our belief into action. What is God asking you to do today? Will you act?

As the Israelite spies prepared themselves to clamber down the wall of Jericho from Rahab's house, they told her to leave the scarlet cord she used to help them escape within her window. It would ensure her security, they explained, along with anyone who happened to be in her home when the Israelites came to the city.

Rahab followed their instructions, securing the red rope in her window. I've often thought, though, that she could simply have left at this point. The Israelites had not yet crossed the Jordan river, Jericho wasn't surrounded yet, we don't hear about the city being shut up with no one able to come in or go out until later in the book of Joshua. Rahab could have gathered her family and left. They could have found somewhere else to settle, another town or city. I think that might have been my reaction – 'we're about to be trapped in a city under siege that we know is going to be defeated. Forget this red cord, let's run away now and save ourselves!'

Sometimes obeying God's instructions doesn't make much sense on the surface. That's why it's so important to believe in him, to understand who he is, because that knowledge assures us that he has our very best in mind. Perhaps Rahab and her family could have escaped the city, but war may have overtaken them somewhere else, with no hope of escape. Alternatively, they may have fled successfully, to Egypt or some other country, but then they would have missed out on God's best. Rahab would never have been brought into the nest of God's own chosen people, would never have given birth to Boaz.

When God's instructions seem to go against what makes sense in our heads, when they seem to go against what would be the easiest path, the most comfortable option for us, we need to hold on to what we believe, and be obedient. Just because we don't understand why God is taking us on a roundabout journey, it doesn't mean he has no plan. God is working in your life, he is working in your circumstances, he is working in the good times and the bad. Follow him. You won't regret it.

It's hard to imagine how Rahab and her family must have felt as the Israelites began to march around the city. We don't know exactly how many were saved. The book of Joshua informs us it was her father and mother, her brothers and sisters and all who belonged to her.[19] They may have been crammed into her little house, watching out of the window, listening to the sound of the trumpets, not daring to leave that home for a moment, in case that was the time when the Israelites would rush in.

On the seventh day, the Israelites march for longer, and suddenly a great rumble sounds about you, and those impenetrable walls of the city of Jericho fall down. They crumble in such a way that the Israelite army can charge in, unhampered by rubble, all aside from one small section – that bit of the wall which contains Rahab's house.

I think I would have felt a bit shaky after that, perhaps concerned this one piece of wall could fall down as well. It would have been a relief to leave, once the battle was done. But leave they did, alive and well, not only Rahab, but her nearest and dearest too. Because of the faith of one woman, the lives of her family were spared.

If you find yourself in the situation where family members or dear friends don't have a relationship with God today, I hope this story encourages you. Your faithfulness will have an impact on their lives, even if you can't see it. Keep holding them in your hearts, keep praying for them, and keep expecting to see God move in their lives.

What a witness it must have been for Rahab's family to see their salvation in such a dramatic way, and all at the hands of the prostitute in the family. It could have been a humbling experience for some of them! Don't ever doubt that the miracles God is working in your life have an impact on those around you. Don't ever believe that the steps of faith you have taken go unnoticed by those who have yet to put their trust in God. God will take those experiences and use them to bring glory to his name.

I love the story of Rahab, how her belief in God combined so beautifully with action to bring salvation to herself and her family. What a wonderful challenge for us today, to believe wholeheartedly, and to live accordingly. Rahab's life was spared because she put her trust in God. Our eternity is assured when we do the same.

Questions for Further Study

Background reading:

Hebrews 11:31
Joshua 2
Joshua 6:22-25

What do we know about Rahab?

What does Hebrews 11:31 tell us that Rahab did by faith?

Why do you think the spies sought refuge in the house of a prostitute?

What were the possible consequences for Rahab in hiding the Israelite spies?

Was it okay for Rahab to lie and disobey the authorities of Jericho to protect the Israelites?

Could there be a situation where this would be acceptable behaviour for us? How can we know?

Hebrews 11:31 talks specifically about Rahab welcoming the spies? What does hospitality have to do with faith?

Read Joshua 2:8-11.

What did Rahab know about the Israelites?

What did she believe about God?

What does all of this tell us about her faith?

Read Joshua 2:15 and Joshua 6:20.

What is the significance of these two verses?

How do you think Rahab and her family would have felt as the walls of Jericho crashed down around them? How would they have felt after?

Read Joshua 6:25.

What was the outcome of Rahab's decision to protect the Israelite spies?

Rahab's action resulted in her family being saved from destruction. How does our faith impact our families and those around us today?

Read Romans 10:9-10.

Through Rahab's belief in the one true God, and her action in shielding the spies, her life was spared. What belief and action do we need for our lives to be saved today?

Read James 2:25.

Considering Rahab's profession, what does this verse tell us about the grace of God?

Look up the following verses. What do they tell us about our salvation?

Psalm 103:10-12	
Psalm 130:3-4	
Isaiah 43:25	
Acts 3:19	

Read Matthew 1:5.

Why do you think Rahab is specifically mentioned in the genealogy of Jesus?

_____

_____

_____

Rahab didn't have her life all together; she wasn't the perfect poster girl for the type of woman we should aspire to be, and yet God used her to help the Israelites to capture Jericho. She was made righteous through her faith, and even ended up being an ancestor of Jesus. What a wonderful example of being saved through faith for us today. As we have faith in Jesus for our own salvation, we know that all our sins are washed away and we are made into completely new creations, ready to use our faith to serve our wonderful God.

CONCLUSION

PERSEVERING IN FAITH

From the worshipper Abel through to the prostitute Rahab, we have met with characters from all walks of life on this exploration of faith. It is wonderful to see how God uses the righteous and the flawed, the strong and the weak to bring about his purposes on this earth. It is amazing to see how even the smallest acts of faith, things that may not have seemed particularly special on the surface, were used to change the course of history. Faith is powerful. It is something we need in every single day of our lives.

> *Now faith is confidence in what we hope for and assurance about what we do not see.*
>
> **-Hebrewa 11:1-**

So many of the characters we have considered found themselves in hopeless situations, where everything they could see was screaming at them to forget the promises of God, to forget God himself. They were commended, because even through those difficult days, even through their moments of doubt, they came out on the other side, confident in God, fully assured they could trust in what they could not see.

It's all too easy to find ourselves looking at the waves, starting to sink, our faith deactivated. I would love to tell you that following

God in your life will always be easy, that you will never need the skills we have identified through these chapters, but that would be a lie. The wonderful truth we can cling to, however, the assurance that may be in opposition to the evidence of our own eyes, is that nothing can overcome God.

> *"In this world you will have trouble. But take heart! I have overcome the world."*
>
> **-John 16:33b-**

This is the wonderful truth to cling to when we are finding it difficult to put our confidence in what we hope for. It is the wonderful truth to cling to when we face the testing of our faith. It is the wonderful truth to cling to in the days where we happily walk with God, and in the days where a promise hoped for remains unfulfilled, and God feels far from us.

The conclusion of the Hebrews 11 Hall of Faith passage is actually found at the start of the following chapter:

> *Therefore, since we are surrounded by such a great cloud of witnesses, let us throw off everything that hinders and the sin that so easily entangles. And let us run with perseverance the race marked out for us, fixing our eyes on Jesus, the pioneer and perfecter of faith. For the joy set before him he endured the cross, scorning its shame, and sat down at the right hand of the throne of God. Consider him who endured such opposition from sinners, so that you will not grow weary and lose heart.*
>
> **-Hebrews 12:1-3-**

Therefore, it begins, following on directly from what we have just finished reading. Therefore, this cloud of witnesses, these very characters we have considered, can spur us on in this race marked out for us. Their example can inspire us and teach us to rid ourselves of those things which may trip us up, which may cause our eyes to waver from Christ Jesus. It takes perseverance. It is not easy, but what good thing ever is? With faith, we can persist, we can remain steadfast, never giving up in spite of what difficulties or setbacks we might face.

We are reminded, in this beautiful conclusion, that it is Jesus who ultimately helps us as we strive to be a people persevering in our journeys of faith. It is he who first awakened faith within us, and it is he who will perfect it. We're not there yet. That work of perfection is ongoing, and there will likely be moments when you fail, when, like Sarah, you laugh, doubting God's promise, doubting his word, perhaps even doubting his goodness. How wonderful to remember, in those moments, that we can always turn to Jesus again. Just as Peter called out from the water, fearing being overwhelmed by the waves that separated him from the Messiah, we can always do the same. And we know he will always reach out a hand to us, pulling us out of the depths. It is impossible to persevere in faith without keeping our eyes fixed on Jesus.

Many of our Hebrews 11 heroes faced difficult times, but none of them come close to the pain and suffering Jesus would face on earth. He endured the cross, he endured the shame of it, the humiliation, the mocking cries of those calling out to him to save himself. He endured opposition, from those he had come to save. He did it all for the joy set before him.

In those moments where we grow weary, in those moments where we lose heart, we can consider our Saviour, and his willingness to put himself through more hardship and torment than we will ever face. Our faith is activated anew as we remember him, and as we remember the joy set before us.

> *My sheep listen to my voice; I know them, and they follow me. I give them eternal life, and they shall never perish; no one will snatch them out of my hand.*
>
> **-John 10:27-28-**

Eternal life is our guarantee, when we put our trust in Jesus. That knowledge is enough to help us through whatever difficulties we may face here and now; it's enough to keep our faith burning bright. No one and nothing can snatch us out of the hand of Jesus. That is an encouraging thought, and one that can help us to persevere, to run this race well.

> *Do you not know that in a race all the runners run, but only one gets the prize? Run in such a way as to get the prize. Everyone who competes in the games goes into strict training. They do it to get a crown that will not last, but we do it to get a crown that will last forever.*
>
> **-1 Corinthians 9:24-25-**

Following Jesus is the best choice for our lives, but it is not the easiest.

Several years ago, I started to follow a fitness programme called Couch to 5k, a system designed to take you from having never run before to being able to run for a solid five kilometres. You start by running for one minute, then walking for a while, then another minute, and so on. Gradually the running times go up and the walking times go down, until suddenly, you realise you can run for far longer than you imagined. It's a good programme, but it was not easy. Spurring myself on to put one foot in front of the other, rather than spending an extra half hour in bed, was a real challenge. Continuing on when my body was shouting at me to stop was incredibly hard work. The sense of satisfaction when I first managed to run for a solid thirty minutes, however, was incredible. It took perseverance, but the feeling of accomplishment I received for completing that goal was fantastic.

It didn't last though. Life got busy and running dropped down the priority list. That temporary crown – increased fitness and improved well-being – faded away. It's hard to persevere, even in the things we know are good for us, but if you're going to persevere in anything, this is the most important thing. We're running this race for a crown that won't fade away, but for one which will last forever. It will take perseverance to keep your faith activated through every storm, but it is worth it. There is so much joy and wonder to come, so very much to look forward to. Remembering the wonder of eternity can make it easier to take each step of faith in our lives here and now.

Rahab isn't actually the final character listed within Hebrews 11, though she's the last we have details about. Instead, the chapter finishes with a long list of people who continued to do great deeds by faith.

> *And what more shall I say? I do not have time to tell about Gideon, Barak, Samson and Jephthah, about David and Samuel and the prophets, who through faith conquered kingdoms, administered justice, and gained what was promised; who shut the mouths of lions, quenched the fury of the flames, and escaped the edge of the sword; whose weakness was turned to strength; and who became powerful in battle and routed foreign armies. Women received back their dead, raised to life again. There were others who were tortured, refusing to be released so that they might gain an even better resurrection. Some faced jeers and flogging, and even chains and imprisonment. They were put to death by stoning; they were sawed in two; they were killed by the sword. They went about in sheepskins and goatskins, destitute, persecuted and mistreated—the world was not worthy of them. They wandered in deserts and mountains, living in caves and in holes in the ground.*
>
> *These were all commended for their faith, yet none of them received what had been promised, since God had planned something better for us so that only together with us would they be made perfect..*
>
> **-Hebrews 11:32-40-**

If the author of the book of Hebrews was seeking to encourage us here, it would be easy to think he had missed the mark. More stories of women receiving their dead back to life and those conquering foreign armies and administering justice, please, and fewer of those who were tortured and persecuted and even killed in brutal ways, refusing to denounce their faith for the sake of a better resurrection.

These people, commended for their faith, did not receive the fulness of all God had promised, because they were all of them born before the days of Jesus. It is only together with us, after Christ's death and resurrection and ascension, that they are truly made perfect and experience the wonder of all that was won at the cross. And yet, they persevered anyway. Without the Holy Spirit living within them, without that advocate and counsellor whom we have access to every day, they persisted, believing that even if they wouldn't see the fulfilment of the promise in their lifetimes, it was coming.

In many countries today, we are free to openly worship and talk about our God, but that is not the case the world over, and it may not always be the case where you live now. There may come a day where you need to make a choice, to pay a price for your faith. It's only as we keep our eyes fixed on Jesus and on that crown that will last forever that we will be able to stand. Even if you never face that particular scenario in your life, it doesn't mean you are any less called to a life of faith. You may not consider your small acts of faith to be particularly ground-shaking, but you have no idea of the lasting impact of your obedience, your perseverance, your willingness to stand firm, and to take the fight to the enemy. You have no idea of the impact your words and your deeds may have on those around you, or on the generations coming after you.

You are called to a life of faith, and right now, at this very moment, you have all the faith you need to move any mountain. You have all the faith you need to stand against whatever this world, or our very real enemy, can throw against you.

We are running a race. It's not always easy, it requires perseverance, but we are surrounded by that crowd of people, those heroes of faith, and they are cheering us on.

> *"The LORD himself goes before you and will be with you; he will never leave you nor forsake you. Do not be afraid; do not be discouraged."*
>
> **-Deuteronomy 31:8-**

Questions for Further Study

It's time to do some digging of your own. The final part of Hebrews 11, from verse 32 on, talks about some other heroes of faith the author didn't have time to get to (Gideon, Barak, Samson, Jephthah, David, Samuel and the prophets). Pick one of these people, or another Bible character who showed faith in their life from the Old or New Testaments, and have a look at their story.

What can we learn from their lives to help us live by faith today?

Who are you studying? Where in the Bible is their story, or the part of the story you are considering, found?

What was their life like?

What did they do by faith?

How did God work through them?

What can we learn from their lesson to apply to our lives today?

Can you think of any other Bible passages that support what you have identified in their life?

I hope you have enjoyed this study in Hebrews 11, and our dig into some of the characters within the Old Testament and their lives of faith.

Are there any characters who really stuck with you after completing this book? Why?

What lessons from the lives of the people within the Hall of Faith have you been able to apply to your own life?

Faith is not always easy. Sometimes it's downright difficult. How wonderful then that we have this amazing cloud of witnesses whom we can consider, and learn lessons from. From Abel through to Rahab, each person has had things to teach us about activating our faith in good situations and bad, and living a life of faith every day. What a wonder that God takes ordinary people, and through them does extraordinary things. As we conclude this study, let's be expectant that through our walk with God we will start to see the extraordinary, and be known as people who lived by faith.

REFERENCES

Introduction – The Adventure of Faith
[1] Luke 17:5
[2] Isaiah 40:31

Abraham – Faith in the Unknown
[3] Matthew 6:8

Abraham – The Testing of Faith
[4] 1 Peter 1:6-7
[5] Isaiah 48:10
[6] 2 Corinthians 11:25-27

Jacob – Faith to Finish Well
[7] Genesis 35:22
[8] John 16:33

Joseph – Faith for the Future
[9] Matthew 6:25-34
[10] Jeremiah 29:11
[11] Ephesians 2:10

Moses' Parents – Faith in the Darkest Days
[12] Luke 22:42-44

Moses – The Comfort of Faith
[13] Genesis 46:34

The Israelites – Faith in the Battle
[14]Ephesians 6:11

Rahab – Saved Through Faith
[15]John 3:16-17
[16]Romans 3:23
[17]Romans 10:9
[18]Psalm 103:12
[19]Joshua 6:23

ABOUT THE AUTHOR

Becky Waterman is a full-time author and Bible teacher, with an international speaking ministry and a YouTube channel, featuring weekly encouragements from the Bible and reaching a worldwide audience.

Since 2017, Becky has lived overseas with her husband, Dave, in the African nations of Uganda and Liberia. As a missionary with Mission Aviation Fellowship, the world's largest humanitarian airline, living in different countries has given Becky the opportunity to expand her teaching ministry, and find new appreciation for the truth of God's Word, applied in vastly different cultures and contexts.

For more information about Becky's ministry, Dave and Becky's missionary journey, free resources for small groups, the latest teaching from Becky's Bible Thoughts online, and much more, you can visit Dave and Becky's website:

www.dbwaterman.com

Printed in Great Britain
by Amazon